COMMON RELIGIOUS TERMS

Upper Saddle River, New Jersey 07458

© 2006 by PEARSON EDUCATION, INC.
Upper Saddle River, New Jersey 07548

ISBN 0-13-170519-9

Printed in the United States of America

Complied with the assistance of Tim J. Davis, Columbus State
Community College, Ohio State University and Otterbein College

A posteriori   Literally means following after and refers to the kind of knowledge that follows and is dependent upon sense experience, as opposed to the kind of knowledge that human reason can know independently of the senses.

A priori   Refers to knowledge that is derived solely from reason independently of the senses. The truth of a priori knowledge is claimed to be both necessary and universal.

Abba   Aramaic term for "father" used by Jesus in addressing God.

Abbasids   Dynasty of classical Islam, ruling at Baghdad, eighth to thirteenth centuries C.E.

Ablutions   Ritual washings, in various traditions.

Abrahamic religions   Religions that claim descent from Abraham as an ancestor (Judaism, Christianity, Islam).

Abu Bakr   Companion of the Prophet Muhammad and first caliph (d. 634).

Adi Buddha   In Tantric Buddhism, the primordial "Buddha without beginning" (Svayambhu), "self-existent," the unitary source of the five celestial Buddhas of the North, South, East, West, and Center.

Adi Granth   "Original collection," The sacred scripture of the Sikhs; see also Guru Granth Sahib.

Adi Granth   Primary collection of Sikh scripture (mostly hymns) assembled by the Fifth Guru: Guru Arjan (1581–1606).

Adoration   Acknowledgment of the sovereignty of the sacred over the individual.

Advaita Vedanta   Philosophy emphasizing nondualism; teaches that all is really Brahman; what appears as other than Brahman is maya, or Brahman's appearance in forms not absolute in themselves.

Advent   In Christianity, refers to the Second Coming of Christ. "Adventist" groups, such as the Seventh Day Adventists, calculate the time of and prepare for the return of Christ. Also, the season of preparation for the celebration of the birth of Christ (Christmas).

Agamas The sacred scriptures of Jainism; believed by some to be the sermons given by Mahavira.

Agape Greek for "love" in Christian New Testament meaning God's love for humans and the selfless love that should bind them. Contrasted with Greek eros, meaning the type of love characterized by longing and desire.

Aggadah The part of the Talmud devoted to folklore.

Agni Vedic god of fire.

Agnosticism From the Greek *a* ("not") and the base of *gignoskein* ("to know"); applies to any proposition (but usually with respect to God) for which evidence for belief or dogmatic unbelief is insufficient.

Ahimsa Noninjury of living beings. This term, found in many Indian religions, was introduced by the Jains. Adherents of ahimsa make every effort to care for all forms of life and seek to avoid injuring or killing any creature.

Ahriman The Pahlavi form of Angra Mainyu.

Ajivakas A determinist and an atheist order of ascetics.

Akhenaton King in ancient Egypt who attempted to enforce a form of monotheism centered on the sun-god Aton.

Akiba ben Joseph (ca. 40–135 C.E.) Founder of a rabbinic school and a specialist in oral law (Halakah), he perfected the midrash style for exposition of the implied meanings in Scripture.

Al-Ghazali Great thinker (1058–1111 C.E.) who synthesized orthodox Islamic thought and Sufism.

'Ali Nephew of the Prophet Muhammad and the fourth caliph (d. 661); considered by Shi'ites to be the first imam or successor to Muhammad.

Allah "The God." The Muslim title for the one sovereign God.

Allahu akbar "God is most great." A frequent expression in Islam.

Al-Qaeda Arabic for "the base." An Islamic terrorist network responsible for the September 11, 2001, attacks and others.

Altar Ancient Hebrew word for "place of sacrifice," or Greek word for "high place." A surface for an offering to God, usually a table in a sanctuary. Frequently has candles, flowers, sacred books, and ritual implements.

Altar of Heaven A huge tiered mountain in Beijing (Peking) where the emperor of China would worship Heaven and Earth at the Winter Solstice and the Summer Solstice, respectively.

Am ha' aretz People of the land, common folk, as distinguished from pious observers of religious practices.

Amaterasu Sun kami Ruler of the Plain of High Heaven, ancestress of the Japanese emperors.

Amida Buddha See Amitabha Buddha.

Amida (Sanskrit: Amitabha) The Buddha of infinite light, the personification of compassion whom the Pure Land Buddhists revere as the intermediary between humanity and Supreme Reality; esoterically, the Higher Self.

Amish The followers of Jacob Ammann (c.a. 1656–1730) in Berne, Switzerland, who broke from the Protestant Swiss Brethren. Under persecution they migrated to Pennsylvania as early as 1727 and spread to Ohio, Indiana, and Ontario, Canada. Noted for their conservative views and lifestyle, the Old Order Amish wear distinctive dress and reject many modern conveniences such as electricity and automobiles.

Amitabha Buddha The Buddha of Pure Land Buddhism; the Buddha of the Western Paradise. It is said that countless ages ago he was an aspirant who, in setting foot on the path of enlightenment, vowed (the "Original Vow") that if he attained full and perfect enlightenment, out of compassion he would bring all who called upon his name into his Buddha paradise. Also known as Emiduo in Chinese and Amida in Japanese.

Amrit The water, sweetened with sugar, used in Sikh baptismal ceremonies.

Amritsar Punjabi city sacred to Sikhs; location of the Golden Temple.

Amulet   An object that is carried on a person or is displayed in a home or place of business to ward off or repel disease, evil, or the assaults of demonic spirits.

Anahita   In Zoroastrianism, one of the Yazata or worshipful ones, the goddess of water and fertility whose cult was widespread in the Roman world.

Ananda   Gautama Buddha's cousin; ananda literally means bliss.

Anatman   No self or no ego. The Buddhist teaching that there is no separate individual human self; humans are instead an impermanent collection of parts, the five skandhas: form, sense, perception, karmic impulses, consciousness.

Ancestor veneration   Archaic theme in indigenous religions that sees dead ancestral spirits present in nature, animals, the heavens, and in newborn children. Requires honoring them and avoiding their displeasure, with home shrines, gravesites, prayers, or sacrifices, to avoid disasters.

Androgynous   From the Greek roots for male and female; denotes the joining of the physical characteristics and the natures of both sexes in one divine or human being.

Anekantwad   The Jain principle of relativity or open-mindedness.

Angel   In the Zoroastrian, Jewish, Christian, and Islamic traditions, an invisible servant of God.

Anglicanism   The post-Reformation term for the Church of England and its daughter churches throughout the world, such as the Episcopal church in the United States; it retains both Catholic and Protestant features.

Angra Mainyu (Ahriman)   "The bad spirit," supreme principle of evil, darkness, and destruction.

Anicca   Pali for "impermanence", the transitoriness of all things. Sanskrit: anitya. Buddhist concept that all reality is constantly changing and without any permanence.

Aniconic   "No images"; referring to traditions which do not encourage visual imagery in religion.

Animism From the Latin *anima*, meaning "soul"; the belief that all things possess a soul or spirit-that is, that all reality is infused with spirits or a spiritual force and is therefore alive. Introduced by E. B. Tylor to refer to what he conceived to be the earliest form of religion.

Annunciation In Christianity, the appearance of an angel to the Virgin Mary to tell her that she would bear Jesus, conceived by the Holy Spirit.

Anthropocentric The view that humans are at the center of creation; the traditional perspective in religions originating in the Middle East (Judaism, Christianity, Islam).

Antinomian From the Greek *anti* ("against") and *nomos* ("law"); describes those religious groups or individuals who hold the doctrine that they are freed from and above the law that remains binding on others. Antinomian sects have threatened Christianity from time to time through the centuries.

Apocalypse From the Greek *apokalypsis*, meaning "revelation"; associated with a class of Jewish and Christian literature that purports to reveal, in highly symbolic language, what is to happen in the future.

Apostle From the Greek for "a person sent forth," one of the twelve disciples of Jesus and Paul, who began their missionary work subsequent to the life of Jesus on earth.

Apostolic succession The doctrine that authority in the Christian church is determined by a line of succession from the apostles of Jesus.

Aquinas, Thomas (c. 1225–1274) Priest and great Western religious philosopher of the Middle Ages in the scholastic tradition of the Catholic Church; influenced by the Aristotelian philosophy of the Muslim thinker Cordova (Averroes), whose works had been discovered by the Christians during the Crusades.

Aranyakas Literally, "forest treatises"; instruction for hermits in Vedic literature.

Arhant One who has obtained complete enlightenment, without becoming a savior of others as a bodhisattva or Buddha; the term especially characteristic of Theravada Buddhism, where the latter vocations are seen as unique to the one Buddha of a world or age.

Arianism   The views promoted by Arius of Alexandria in the fourth century that Christ was a created being, "made" at a point in time and not coeternal with God—a heresy ruled out in the Creed of Nicaea by the phrases "begotten not made" and "of one substance with the Father."

Arjuna   Major character in the Bhagavad Gita. The warrior in the Bhagavad Gita. instructed by Krishna.

Ark of the Covenant   The portable chest in Hebrew tradition (known also in other ancient cultures) containing two tablets on which were written the Ten Commandments (Deut.10). In Judaism, the shrine containing God's commandments to Moses. It was seen as a powerful manifestation of the presence of God. It was taken to Jerusalem by David and then installed in the Temple by Solomon (I Kings 8).

Armageddon   Literally, "Mount Megiddo." Designates the final battle associated with the coming of the end time.

Arminianism   Belief that one has free will to decide for or against faith in Christ, in contrast to a strict Calvinist view of Divine election and predestination.

Aryan Invasion Theory   Speculation originally advanced by Western scholars that the Vedas were written by people invading India rather than by people already there.

Ascetic   Generally refers to a person who lives an austere and self-denying life. In many religions, refers to a special group of devotees who lead a life of contemplation and self-denial, such as monks or hermits in order to prepare oneself for receiving enlightenment, God's will, God's love, etc..

Asceticism   The institutionalization of ascetics' practices.

Ash`arism   The immensely influential school of Muslim theology that emphasizes that the ways of God are beyond human understanding; human knowledge of God, it says, can only be based on revelation.

Ashkenazi   Jews from Northern and Eastern Europe. Originally, "Ashkenazi" referred to Jews of Germany and France. However, in 1182 the Jews were expelled from France. Many moved to Spain and Poland, as well as Germany. Their special language, Yiddish, developed primarily in Germany and Poland, and their religious practices also were influenced by the cultures of those countries. While Ashkenazi Jewry is generally considered to be of German descent, the real center became Poland, but eventually spread throughout Europe. Most Jews in the United States are Ashkenzi.

Ashoka   First Mauryan emperor of India in 273 B.C.E. who instituted reforms along Buddhist lines, such as moral education.

Ashramas   One of the four "stages of life" in Hinduism. The practice of withdrawal from the world in which one lives as a holy recluse; an ashram is a community dwelling place where those who have withdrawn can gather around a guru, or teacher, to study and meditate.

Ashtoreth   Hebrew name in Torah for widespread third-millennium goddess also known as Asherah, a Canaante goddess symbolized by a pillar or tree, opposed by Hebrew monotheistic priests. Similar to Ishtar and Innana, Sumerian, Assyrian and Babylonian Goddesses of love, fertility and war. Often a generic term for fertility goddesses, counterpart of the baalim, fertility gods.

Asvamedha   The ancient Aryan horse sacrifice.

Atharva Veda   The fourth book in the Vedic collection, containing rituals and prayers used in the worship of Aryan gods.

Atheism   The assertion that there is no God, or belief that there is no deity.

Atonement   Especially prominent in Judaism and Christianity; a representative sacrifice of the life of a victim (symbolized by its outpoured blood), to serve as an expiation for an individual or a community to cover an offense to God or gods.

Augustine   A North African bishop of the late fourth and early fifth centuries. He converted from Roman paganism to Christianity and became one of the most influential Christian writers. He was later beatified as a saint. His work had particular influence on Martin Luther and, therefore, Protestantism specifically.

Avalokitesvara (Avalokita)   The bodhisattva of compassion. As male in Tibet (Chenrezig), watches over people and is incarnate in the Dalai Lama. Female in China and Japan.

Avatara   In Hinduism, the concept of earthly incarnation of a deity, such as Vishnu, who came to earth in many forms to save humans, most notably Krishna.

Avesta   The sacred scriptures of Zoroastrians, including the Yasna (the Gathas), the Yashts, and other sacred texts.

Avidya   Hindu term for "ignorance" in the Upanishads; mistaking maya for reality.

Awqaf (pl.)   Religious endowments for "work pleasing to Allah," usually for aid to the poor or for support of schools.

Axial Age   Term originally coined by historian Karl Jaspers but used differently by others following him, which denotes a period of many parallels among the civilizations of the world, especially in religion, during the period of approximately 900 B.C.E. to 600 C.E. The term itself is controversial as, originally at least, it was claimed that Jesus was the "axial" (i.e., the center around which all else turns) and, therefore, the term implied a particular Western perspective on world history not necessary accepted by others.

Ayatollah   In Shi`ite Islam, a legal and religious teacher regarded as possessing very great learning and righteousness, whose authority is believed to be backed by that of the infallible hidden Imam.

Baal "Lord" or "master," a nature deity common to the Western Semitic world; sometimes the title of a local deity: Baal-hazor or (fem.) Baalat-beer.

Babylonian Captivity of the Church Period between 1309 and 1377 C.E., when the papacy of the Roman Catholic Church was at Avignon, France.

Baha'i New religious movement arising in Persia and spreading through the world, founded by Baha'u'llah (1817–1892), regarded by his followers as the Manifestation of God for this new world era.

Baptism Ritual of initiation into the Christian church through washing of water, viewed as a sacrament by many.

Bar Kochba "Son of the star"—a messianic appellation— leader of the "Second Rebellion," 132–135 C.E., against Hadrian.

Bar mitzvah Means "Son of the Commandment"; applied to a Jewish boy on his thirteenth birthday when, in a synagogue ceremony, he takes on his religious responsibilities in the community. The boy thereafter has certain prerogatives, such as the reading of the Torah, is held accountable for his own sins, and is commanded to fast on the Day of Atonement.

Barakah In Islamic mysticism, the spiritual wisdom and blessing transmitted from master to pupil.

Bardo Tibetan Buddhist "in between" realms of existence, such as life, dreams, and death. Numerous forms of gods, ghosts and demons appear with many expressions of earthy passions, but each can be dissolved into its primordial Buddha-nature.

Bardo Thodol The Tibetan Book of the Dead, with instructions for the intermediate state (bardo).

Basho Seventeenth-century Japanese Zen monk, best known for his haiku poetry.

Bat mitzvah Equivalent of bar mitzvah ceremony for girls in Reform and Conservative Jewish congregations.

Beatitudes First ten verses of Jesus' Sermon on the Mount.

Benares One of the seven sacred cities of India, a center of pilgrimage for many. Devoted to Siva, god of generation and destruction. Many sick and elderly Hindus go there to die and be cremated.

Bhagavad-Gita Sanskrit for "Song of the Lord"; a section of the Mahabharata. Regarded by many as the crowning achievement of Hindu literature, synthesizing the major strands within Hindu teaching.

Bhakti Sanskrit for "devotion"; the path to God or liberation in Hinduism that stresses love and devotion to a deity rather than study or ritual obligation. The way of devotion is classically outlined in the *Bhagavad-Gita*.

Bhakti Yoga "Devotional Yoga"; the Hindu practice of seeking liberation and union with the Divine through loving, often ecstatic devotion to one of the personified dieties. Presented in the Bhagavad Gita and other texts.

Bhikshu (Pali: bhikkhu; feminine: bhikshuni or bhikkhuni) A Buddhist monk or nun who renounces worldliness for the sake of following the path of liberation and whose simple physical needs are met by lay supporters.

Biblical criticism The modern interpretation of the Christian Bible using modern historical, archaeological and literary tools to analyze how the Bible came into being. It began in Germany in the 19th century, showing many biblical texts to be edited compilations and even contradictory (as in the two Genesis creation accounts). This provoked a stormy reaction among fundamentalists and orthodox who wanted to retain a literal interpretation.

Bodhi Tree (Sanskrit: "Tree of the Awakening") The tree in India under which Siddhartha Gautama achieved enlightenment (nirvana). Also called "Bo" Tree.

Bodhidharma Legendary Buddhist monk in the Indian Dhyanic tradition who is credited with having brought a particular form of meditative Buddhism to China during the late fifth or early sixth century C.E. His teachings and influence are said to have greatly inspired the development of Zen (Chan) Buddhism in China.

Bodhisattva In Buddhism a person who has achieved great spiritual wisdom but instead of accepting nirvana chooses to stay behind to assist others in their quest of enlightment.

Bön The Pre-Buddhist indigenous religion of Tibet, blended with Buddhism.

Boxer Rebellion The "Boxers" was the name given by foreigners to members of a secret society in China known as the Fists of Righteous Harmony, practitioners of martial arts. The Boxers were recruited by the Empress Dowager Tsu Hsi to rid China of foreigners and foreign influences, which had forced the Chinese government to make humiliating concessions in furtherance of foreign trade. In 1900, this resulted in a "rebellion" during which foreign diplomats and their families were placed under siege by the Boxers and repeatedly attacked for two months. The foreign diplomats and their families were rescued by international Western military forces, which subdued the Boxers and the Chinese imperial forces and destroyed the power of the Ching Dynasty.

Brahma One of the three important gods in Hindu worship, generally regarded as the creator of the world.

Brahman Hindu term for ultimate reality; the divine source and pervading essence of the universe.

Brahmin A priest or member of the priestly caste in Hinduism.

Buddha An enlightened being; also used to refer to the historical Buddha, Siddhartha Gautama.

Buddha nature The Mahayana Buddhist concept that all reality is infused with Buddhahood.

Buddhism A way of thought and practice that emphasizes moral practice, meditation, and enlightenment founded by Siddhartha Gautama, the Buddha, in India during the sixth century B.C.E.

Buddhism, major branches 1. *Mahayana:* stresses ethical activity in the world, including Zen, a meditative school in Japan (Chan in China) 2. *Theravada:* stresses more monastic discipline and individual liberation, 3. *Vajrayana:* Tibetan, rich in imagery and colorful ritual, follow Dalai Lama; 4. *Amitabha* ("Immeasurable life"): a celestial field of bliss— "Pure Land" in Japan, and others.

Burning Bush While tending Jethro's flock on Mount Horeb (Sinai), in tradition, Moses heard the voice of God in a fire in a bush, burning but not consuming the bush. There God called Moses to lead the Hebrews out of Egyptian slavery (Ex. 3–4).

 **Bushido** "Way of the warrior, " the Japanese code of self-discipline for warriors, based on Zen, Shinto, and Neo-Confucian ideals.

Busk Festival at the green corn ripening among the Creek Native Americans.

Butsudan In Japan, Buddhist altar in the home.

Caliph From khalifa (literally, "deputy," "representative"); successors of Muhammad in leading Islam. At first, the caliphate was limited to the companions of the Prophet Muhammad, but as Islam grew, the caliphate took on the role of a dynastic political leadership.

Calvinism Expression of Protestant Christianity that traces its doctrines and practices to the teachings of the Reformer John Calvin (1509–1564). These include the sovereignty of God, election or predestination, original sin, the irresistibility of grace, and a deep sense of calling in our secular occupation.

Canaanites Inhabitants of the land promised to the patriarchs (boundaries uncertain-in the Bible, usually west of the Jordan); not a homogeneous population, but mostly Semitic.

Canon Originally, "measuring reed"; the list of authoritative scriptures in a particular tradition. a collection of sacred writings deemed authoritative by and for a religious group.

Canonization Roman Catholic process by which the Pope officially accepts a person as a saint.

Cao Dai A spiritualistic and syncretistic new religious movement in Vietnam.

Cargo Cults Melanesian movements in expectation of the return of the ancestors on great cargo ships, a response to Western influence.

Caste (*Jati:* "species" or *Varna:* "color") Hindu hierarchical social class distinction on the basis of heredity, ritual, or occupation: *Brahmana* (priests), *Kshatriya* (warrior), *Vaishya* (merchants) *Shudra* (servant). There are numerous sub-castes, such as *Tawaif* (dancing girl). Outcastes or *untouchables* have no caste and do the most undesirable work, such as garbage collection. Marriage and eating together are forbidden between castes.

Casting the circle In Wicca, a ritual used to create sacred space.

Catacombs Underground cemeteries, such as the early Christian catacombs of Rome. Catacombs were all over the Roman world, especially in Europe and were used by the Polytheists as well.

Catharsis A cleansing or a purging; in religion, one important function is the act of purification that is necessary if we are to be right with or in the presence of the sacred. Also serves to purge the emotions.

Cathedral A large church that is the seat or office of the Bishop who leads many churches in a Roman Catholic or Anglican (England) / Episcopal (U.S.) Diocese, or region.

Catholic Christian churches referring to themselves as Catholic claim to be the representatives of the ancient undivided Christian church.

Celestial Kingdom In the cosmology of the Church of Jesus Christ of Latter-day Saints, the highest of the three levels of heaven.

Ch'ondogyo An important new religious movement in Korea that has advocated worship of the God of Heaven, a combination of features of all major Korean spiritual traditions, and of social reform.

Chador A covering from head to toe worn by women in Islamic countries with strict practices. The practice of wearing the chador is called "veiling." The burqua is a more severe version.

Chakras In some yogic teaching, centers of spiritual power along the spinal column, which can be opened by raising the kundalini.

Chan Chinese Buddhist tradition, influenced by Taoism, stresses meditation, master/disciple relations, and nature; became Zen in Japan.

Changing Woman Important divine figure among Native Americans of southwestern North America.

Chanoyu The art of the Japanese tea ceremony; also called chado, "the way of tea."

Chanukah (Hanukkah) Minor Jewish holiday. A joyous event commemorating the relighting of the lamps of the holy temple in the year 165 C.E., during the campaign of the Maccabee brothers to drive out the oppressor.

Charismatics In Christianity, refers to groups, individuals, churches that emphasize the role of the Holy Spirit manifest in ecstatic gifts like speaking in tongues.

Chi Chinese word for the inner biological/spiritual energy of nature, including that found in human beings. It is chi that is invoked in martial arts and is manipulated in acupuncture.

Ch'i-kung A Taoist system of harnessing inner energies for spiritual realization.

Chinvat Bridge Persian Zoroastrian image where dead souls cross river to paradise; becomes impossibly narrow so sinners fall into stinky waters, but wide for those going to paradise.

Christ Greek title meaning "anointed one" from Hebrew "messiah," applied to Jesus of Nazareth by his followers.

Christian Identity Radical American Fundamentalist groups who seek to merge Christianity and the state into a theocratic society ruled by religious laws. It is deeply anti-Semitic and recently has been centered on the Aryan compound in Idaho.

Christianity, major branches 1. *Eastern Orthodox:* centered in Constantinople/Istanbul, strong in Russia, Greece Balkan states. Rejects Pope, reveres icons, allows no women priests. 2. *Roman Catholic:* Led by Pope in Rome, requires male celibate priests. 3. *Protestant:* Began with Martin Luther in 1517 C.E., sees Bible as main authority, all believers have direct access to God, women may be ministers. Denominations: Baptists, Methodists, Lutherans, Presbyterians, Anglicans/Episcopalians, Quakers, and many more.

Christology Doctrine about the nature and role of Christ.

Church A socially recognized religious organization which makes its appeal to all members of a society, which has a stake in the well-being of the larger society, and which claims to be the custodian of religious truth.

Church of Christ Scientist Christian group founded in America by Mary Baker Eddy (1821–1910), emphasizing reliance on Divine Mind for spiritual growth and for overcoming sickness.

Circumcision Boys' initiation ritual in many indigenous societies, in Islam, and in Judaism; in Judaism it occurs on the eighth day after birth and is called brit milah ("covenant of circumcision").

Civil Religion　A term used to encompass the symbols, ideas and myths, and ritual-like practices of a society that legitimize social and political institutions. In a society such as found in the United States, this may include religious and secular elements.

Common Era　Years after the traditional date used for the birth of Jesus, previously referred to in exclusively Christian terms as ad and now abbreviated to C.E. as opposed to B.C.E. ("before Common Era").

Communion/Eucharist　A Christian sacrament, or sacred ritual of serving wine and bread as the body and blood of Jesus Christ, or in memory of him.

Compensation　A psychological term that refers to the human tendency to substitute an area of strength for an area of weakness. Some people argue that belief in God is compensation for human finitude and limitation.

Confirmation　A Christian sacrament by which awareness of the Holy Spirit is enhanced.

Confucius ("Kong Fuzi" in Chinese)　One of the most influential men in Chinese history and philosophy. His name is associated with the Confucian Classics, and in his name there evolved a whole system for organizing and conducting Chinese society, based on the idea of li (ritual).

Conservative Judaism　Movement attempting to adapt Judaism to modern life by using principles of change within the traditional laws; occupies middle ground between Reform and Orthodox Judaism.

Constantine　Roman emperor (ca. 307–337 C.E.) who legalized and promoted Christianity.

Consubstantiation　The belief that in the sacrament of Holy Communion the body and blood of Christ are actually present with or alongside (but not replacing) the physical elements of bread and wine. Belief held by many Lutherans.

Contagious magic　A form of sympathetic magic based on the view that things once conjoined continue to influence each other when separated; thus magic performed on a lock of hair may affect the person from whom it came.

Conversion　The process of deliberate change from one religion to another.

Copt Member of the traditional Monophysite Christian church originating and centering in Egypt; the Coptic church traces its history to the earliest Christian communities.

Cosmogony Refers to those stories or theories that have to do with the birth or creation of the world or universe.

Cosmological proof One of the classical proofs of the existence of God arguing that the world is not self-explanatory and requires an infinite (noncontingent) being, God, as its explanation. The contingency of the world requires a first cause, a necessary being.

Cosmology Derived from the Greek words meaning "doctrine of the world"; the study of (or a view of) how the universe (all reality) is ordered. Has to do with the branch of philosophical or scientific speculation that deals with the origin and structure of the world.

Council of Chalcedon In 451 C.E., the fourth ecumenical council of the Catholic church, which was held to oppose the heresy that Jesus was of two natures or personalities, one Divine and one human, and to reassert the orthodox doctrine of the church that Jesus is both Divine and human in one unified personality and nature.

Council of Ephesus In 431 C.E., the third ecumenical council of the Catholic church, which was held to oppose the heresy that Jesus was not God when born of Mary and to reassert the orthodox doctrine of the church that Jesus was both God and man when born of Mary, and, therefore, that Mary can be called Theotokos, God-bearer.

Council of Nicaea In 325 C.E., the first ecumenical council of the Catholic church, called by Emperor Constantine, to resolve certain doctrinal matters that were in dispute in the Catholic church, to settle disputes about the nature of Christ; the result was the Nicene Creed, which sets out the standard doctrine that, among other things, Jesus was the only begotten son of the Father (God), is of the same substance as the Father, and suffered and died for the sins of humankind.

Council of Trent In 1545–1563 C.E., the nineteenth ecumenical council, which was held to address the heresies of the Protestants and to reform the Catholic church.

Covenant An agreement characterized by mutual loyalty and trust. In Judaism and Christianity, refers to pacts between God and his chosen people.

Coven   The small groups into which Wiccans are informally organized, and in which rituals are performed.

Creed   A formal statement of the beliefs of a particular religion.

Cro-Magnon   Early humans; the Cro-Magnons lived from approximately 25,000 to 7000 B.C.E.

Crucifixion   The common method for executing dissidents in Rome; involved nailing the condemned's hands and feet to a structure made of two crossed beams set upright in the ground, thereby leaving the condemned to die a slow, agonizing death.

Crusades   Attempts by Christians of western Europe to recapture the Holy Land by force.

Cult   A term used by sociologists to denote a minority religion characteristically centered on a charismatic leader, who requires strict adherence to the beliefs and practices of the group. Generally, the cult combines teachings and practices from several sources and often requires adherents to sever ties with people who are not a part of the cult.

Cultural Revolution   The period from 1966 to 1976 in China during which fanatical Red Guards attempted to destroy all forms of "old" religion and culture.

Curia   The "Roman Curia" consists of the people who assist the Pope of the Catholic church; they are from a consortium of departments and institutes, including the Secretariat of State, congregations, tribunals, pontifical councils, and other offices.

Daevas   Gods, celestial beings; in Zoroastrian usage, demons given to malice and corruption.

Dafa   In Falun Gong teaching, the "great law of the universe."

Daijo-sai   In Japan, the harvest festival as celebrated by the emperor after his accession to the throne.

Daimon   A spirit full of mana, often an inward mentor, a source of inspiration and a moral guardian to an individual.

Dakhmas   "Towers of silence," enclosures open to the sky within which corpses are left to be picked clean by vultures.

Dalai Lama   "Ocean of wisdom"; the title of the chief spiritual and temporal leader of the Tibetan people. The current (fourteenth) Dalai Lama is Tenzin Gyatso.

Dao   The mysterious, unnameable cosmic power that is the source and end of all reality according to philosophical Daoism.

Dao de jing (Tao te ching)   The book purportedly written by Laozi, the legendary founder of Daoism. "Dao de jing" means something like "The Book of the Dao and How to Apply Its Strength."

Daoist Popes   The direct decendents of Zhang, called "Heavenly Teacher," who said that Laozi, the legendary founder of Daoism, had appeared to him from the realm of spirits and had given him a sword and other apparatus with which he was able to exercise control over the spiritual world. In the past, they exercised a tenuous spiritual authority over Daoist priests in the southern part of China.

Dar al-Islam   "Abode of Islam"; Territories of the ummah under Muslim control, whereas the rest of the world is the Dar al-Harb, "abode of warfare" a symbol of the ideal of political unity established by submission to the will of Allah.

Darsan   Visual contact with the divine through encounters with Hindu images or gurus.

Dasturs   Hereditary order of Zoroastrian high priests.

Davening   In Hasidic Judaism, prayer.

De   Inherent power, the authority of authentic character and virtue.

Deacon Literally, "servant," "attendant," "minister"; a functionary in Christian churches.

Decalogue The Ten Commandments in the biblical book of Exodus 20.

Deism From the Latin *deus* ("god"); applies to a movement of thought in the seventeenth and eighteenth centuries in Europe that held a belief in one God who creates the world but who does not intervene directly in its ongoing functioning. God allows the world to operate by the natural laws he originally established. The deist God is a transcendent Creator but is not immanent in the world.

Deity yoga In Tibetan Buddhism, the practice of meditative concentration on a specific deity.

Demiurge Derived from a Greek word for "handyman" or "tinkerer" who fashioned articles out of materials supplied by customers. When applied to the notion of a creator-god, it refers to the view that the creator fashioned a cosmos out of available materials but did not create those materials. This kind of creator was suggested by the ancient Greek philosopher Plato and by John Stuart Mill in the nineteenth century.

Dengyo Daishi Originally Saicho (762-822), he brought the teachings of the Tiantai school of Buddhism in China to Japan, which became Tendai Buddhism there and which holds that the Lotus Sutra is the culminating expression of the Buddha's teachings.

Denomination A form of religious institution distinctive of Protestant Christianity and often contrasted with both state-established churches and religious sects. Common in pluralistic societies like the United States where no church is established by law or privileged by the state and each religious group receives equal treatment before the law. Resemble churches in that they are usually large and inclusive across socioeconomic lines, and their members are not alienated from the larger society.

Deontological From the Greek, "that which is binding"; refers to an approach to ethics based on duties.

Dervish Literally, "doorway" or "one who comes to the door"; The "whirling dervishes" (the Mevlevi Order) were founded by Jelaluddin Mevlana Rumi, who was a mystic and a poet. Wearing long white robes with wide skirts, the dervishes do a whirling dance, which is believed to bridge the material and spiritual worlds.

Deus absconditus ("Concealed god") Latin for god whose mysterious depth is obscured by rationalist, speculative attempts to define the nature of god, thus turning god into another "thing."

Deus otiosus ("Hidden god") Latin for a creator god who, after making the world, withdraws from it, leaving it to lesser spirits or to humanity.

Devi Sanskrit for "goddess." In Hinduism, various devi are worshipped.

Devotionalism Emphasis on deeply felt prayer and meditation, i.e., devoting oneself to the Divine, however conceived in various religions.

Dhammapada A collection of short sayings attributed to Buddha.

Dharma In Hinduism, the social/cosmic order, social duty, and proper behavior; which works for righteousness in accordance with rita, the cosmic order, and to which the righteous adhere; also one's own duty. In Buddhist usage, the truth; the teaching of the Buddha, which are related to the cosmic order; dharmas also refer to the constituents of all phenomena.

Dharmakaya The expression of the Buddha-nature as the essence of the universe, a term and meaning really identical in Mahayana with Nirvana or the Void. Called the Clear Light of the Void in The Tibetan Book of the Dead.

Dhikr ("Remembrance") Spiritual exercises in Sufism focusing the consciousness on God.

Dhimmi A person of a non-Muslim religion whose right to practice that religion is protected within an Islamic society.

Diaspora Literally, "dispersion." Refers to many widely dispersed communities as opposed to having a center location for a people. In Judaism, specifically, it refers to the Jewish people who have been dispersed throughout the world because of persecution; however, the term is also applied to others with similar fates, e.g., the Tibetan Buddhists, whose leader, the Dalai Lama, has met with Jewish leaders to discuss ways to continue religious and cultural identity in "diaspora."

Dietary law Jewish laws pertaining to the proper preparation and eating of food, and the avoidance of certain animal food; see kashrut.

Digambara Literally, "clothed in air," a sect of Jainism in southern India.

Divali Hindu festival of lights and good fortune that welcomes the new year, also celebrated by Jains.

Divination Methods of discovering the nature and significance of events, usually future ones.

Divine kingship Notion in many ancient societies, such as Egypt and Mesopotamia, that the king represents divine power to the human realm.

Divine Mind In Christian Science, the name for God.

Docetism Teaching by some in the early church that Christ only appeared to be human.

Doctrine Statements of the basic beliefs of a religion.

Dogen Important thinker (1200–1253) and founder of Soto Zen in Japan.

Dogma A system of beliefs declared to be true by a religion.

Dong Zhongshu A very influential Chinese thinker (c. 179–104 B.C.E.) who developed the Han Synthesis, which combined aspects Daoism and Confucianism.

Dreaming Time Mythic time of the beginnings in Australian tradition.

Dualism Any explanation offered in terms of two equal but opposed powers, principles, or beings. A religious view is dualistic when it suggests that there are two equal but opposed deities, one evil and one good, one material, one spiritual. Such a view is found in Zoroastrian religion. A metaphysical dualism is that of body and soul or matter and spirit.

Dukkha Pali for "suffering." The term used in Buddhism for life's inevitable suffering. According to Buddhist belief, suffering caused by craving is the condition from which humans need to be liberated.

Durga Hindu Goddess, a gentle and beautiful, golden-colored goddess popular in Bengal, wife of Shiva, with many arms, appearing in many forms, often riding a lion or tiger and having the fierce capacities of a warrior who fought giants and demons.

Easter   Christian holy day on Sunday in the spring celebrating the resurrection of Jesus Christ three days after his crucifixion.

Eastern Orthodoxy   A family of ancient Christian churches centered in Eastern Europe and the Middle East, divided into autonomous national bodies, that is, Greek Orthodox, Russian Orthodox, and so on. Desceneded from the church of the Byzantine Wmpire, they are characterized by ornate ritual, rich spirituality, and doctrinal conservatism.

Ecofeminism   Contemporary movement that identifies patriarchal values as the cause of the ecological crisis and proposes ecological wholeness through feminist values.

Ecstasy   In religion, a powerful alteration of consciousness, or trance believed to open the soul to inspired spiritual experience or possession.

Ecumenical   From the Greek for "the whole inhabited world"; in Christianity, used to refer to the movement for increased cooperation and unity among Christian churches.

Ecumenism   Rapprochement between branches of Christianity or among all faiths.

Edict of Milan   The edict of Constantine in 313 C.E., which declared that it was no longer legal to persecute Christians.

Eightfold Path   Right understanding, thought, speech, action, livelihood, effort, mindfulness, and concentration or samadhi-the fundamental ideals of Buddhist life and practice as taught by the Buddha.

Eisai   Founder (1141–1215) of Rinzai Zen in Japan.

Elohim   A name for God in Hebrew Scripture; although a plural form, it is taken to refer to the "One who is All" as distinguished from elelim, "nongods" or idols. In the International Raelian Religion, the elohim are "those who came from the sky" in a flying saucer to teach humanity.

El-Shaddai ("Deity of the mountains")   A name for God, especially as the God of the covenant with Abraham.

Emergence myth   Story of original people emerging from lower worlds into the present world, as among the Navajo.

Enlightenment   The realization of truth that liberates.

Ennead   The group of nine gods headed by the creator Atum, worshiped at Heliopolis in ancient Egypt.

Enuma   Elish epic of creation in ancient Babylon, read during new year festival.

Epiphany   From the Greek, meaning "manifestation" of a god or divine power. In Christianity, the recognition of Jesus's spiritual kingship by the three Magi. The feast of Epiphany, or Manifestation of Christ, is celebrated on January 6.

Epistemology   The theory of knowledge; an inquiry into the origin, validity, and limits of knowledge.

Epistles   Formal letters.

Eschatology   From the Greek *eschatos*, meaning the "last things"; the understanding of nature, of human life, and of history in terms of their goals or destinies. Often associated with beliefs concerning life after death, judgment, and Heaven and Hell resurrection, reincarnation, end of the known world.

Essenes   Monastic Jewish community whose primary headquarters may have been Wadi Qumran near the Dead Sea. They existed mainly during the first century B.C.E. and the first century C.E. and were extremely interested in eschatology.

Ethics   Thought and study about moral decisions, on the basis of traditions of right and wrong.

Etiological   Used in religion to designate those doctrines or myths that describe and explain the origin of something-for example, the world, human institutions, or beliefs.

Eucharist   Literally, "thanksgiving"; Christian memorial meal of bread and wine that celebrates the sacrifice of Jesus.

Evangelical   Term widely used to refer to those forms of Protestantism that emphasize the supreme authority of Scripture and salvation by faith—sometimes expressed by a powerful conversion experience (rather than on becom-

ing a Christian through birth or baptism)—in the atonement of Jesus; also, sometimes connotes "evangelizing," that is, spreading the "good news" of the Gospels to others.

Exclusivism   The idea that one's own religion is the only valid way.

Excommunication   Exclusion from participation in the Christian sacraments (applied particularly to Roman Catholicism), which is a bar to gaining access to heaven.

Exegesis   The analysis of a passage of a text, in this case sacred texts, in an effort to understand or to offer commentary on the meaning of the passage. Exegesis involves examining many questions regarding the text, such as its historical and literary context, the lexical or correct understanding of the words, its grammar, structure, and form or genre, its audience, and so on.

Exile   The Jewish captivity in Babylon, especially the period from the fall of Jerusalem in 586 B.C.E. until the first return to Jerusalem in 538 B.C.E.

Existential   Those beliefs or actions that focus on personal existence in contrast to those matters that are impersonal or indifferent to the person. Existentialism is concerned with protesting against positions that view the person as an object of purely rational or scientific analysis. It emphasizes the "subjective"—things such as finitude, guilt, suffering, and death that cannot be approached in the manner of scientific problem solving—and the ambiguities of life that arise from our unique human freedom.

Exodus   The escape of the ancient Hebrews from slavery in Egypt, around 1250 B.C.E., led by Moses through the Sinai peninsula to the Promised Land, now Israel.

Exorcist   Priest or magician who practices exorcism, or the expelling of evil spirits by the use of a special ritual or formula or the use of a holy name.

Expiation   Making right by some ritual act or offering for the injury or sin done to some other person or god; closely related to atonement and propitiation, expiation involves an act of sacrifice to remove pollution or sin.

Extreme unction   Roman Catholic last rite given to the dying.

Fa-jia The School of Laws or models (fa), Legalism.

Fakir ("Poor man") An Indian ascetic who performs magic or feats of endurance. In Sufism, a seeker of the way to union with Allah.

Fana Sufi term for mystical absorption in the Divine.

Fatiha The first sura of the Qur'an.

Fatwa In Islam, a formal opinion treating a moral, legal, or doctrinal question, issued by a recognized scholar.

Female genital mutilation (FGM) The disfiguring and/or removal of female sexual organs as part of a rite of passage for girls. Particularly common in Africa.

Feminist Spirituality Movement Contemporary movement in many religious traditions emphasizing feminine aspects of the sacred and a recovery of feminine values in spiritual practices and in human relationships.

Feng liu In Daoism, "wind and stream"; a metaphor for spontaneity, acting according to the movement of what is happening day by day.

Feng-shui An elaborate art that involves determining the Yang-Yin "bearings" of locations for houses, businesses, tombs, and temples, as well as the arrangements of rooms and the objects within them.

Fetish Derived from the Portuguese *feitico*, meaning "skillfully made"; in religion, refers to various objects, either natural or artificial, that are endowed with supernatural magical power or virtue and are capable of averting evil or bringing good nature (rabbit's foot, lucky item, religious charm).

Fideism From the Latin *fides*, meaning "faith"; associated with those who believe that faith must precede reason with regard to knowledge of God and that reason alone is incapable of producing genuine knowledge of God. Fideism is the opposite of rationalism.

Filial Piety Important aspect of Confucian society. It refers to the obligation of a son to negate his own feelings and individuality in deference to the wishes and pleasure of his father.

Filioque ("And from the Son") A clause emphasizing the equality of the Persons of the Trinity (the Spirit "proceeds from the Father and from the Son"); St. Augustine urged it, and it found its way into Latin versions of the Creed of Chalcedon, much to the distress of the Greek Orthodox Church.

Fire Temple Main worship sanctuary for Zoroastrians, where the sacred fire is kept burning.

First Council of Buddhism Held at Rajagriha shortly after the Buddha's parinirvana, where, according to tradition, the Buddha's sayings were recited and compiled.

Five Classics The heart of the Confucian scriptures, including the Shujing (Classic of History), the Shijing (Classic of Poetry), the Yijing (I Ching, Classic of Changes), the Lijing (Classic of Rites), and the Chunqiu (Spring and Autumn Annals).

Five Elements Chinese idea of five modes of energy in the universe that mutually influence each other: wood, fire, earth, metal, water.

Five main virtues Confucianism emphasizes moderating emotions to reach psychih and social harmony. The five main virtues that cultivate such harmony are: courtesy, magnanimity, good faith, diligence, and goodness.

Five Pillars of Islam 1. Creed: (*Shahada*): There is only one God, Allah, and Muhammed is his prophet. 2. Prayer (*Salat*): Pray five times a day, 3. Almsgiving (*Zakat*): Free-will gifts to needy, 4. Fasting during month of *Ramadan*, 5. Pilgrimage (*Hajj*): Journey to Mecca.

Five Precepts The basic Buddhist moral precepts, to refrain from destroying life, from taking what is not given, from wrongful sexual behavior, from wrongful speech, and from drugs and liquor.

Five relationships, The In Confucianism, society is believed to be based on these five relationships: (1) ruler and subject, (2) father and son, (3) husband and wife, (4) elder and younger brother, and (5) friend and friend.

Four Noble Truths The basic teaching of Buddhism, expressed by Siddartha Gautama in his Deer Park Sermon: (1) life is painful; (2) the cause of this suffering is desire; (3) there is a way to overcome this suffering; (4) the way is the eightfold path.

Four Sights   Sickness, old age, death, and a wandering hermit; seeing these motivated Siddhartha Gautama to seek enlightenment.

Fravashi   Originally one of the immortal parts of human beings, the preexistent ancestral soul; later, a guardian genius associated with gods as well as humans.

Friday Mosque   A mosque large enough to hold the entire population of a community, designated as the place for its Friday noon service.

Fundamentalism   A movement within a religion that stresses the absolute, unchanging, and unequivocally true nature of the movement's core teachings. First used to refer to a movement in Christianity; now frequently applied to movements in other religions.

Gahambars Zoroastrian seasonal feasts dedicated to the creation of heaven, water, earth, trees, animals, and humans.

Gaia The Greek name for the earth goddess. The Gaia Principle (developed by James Lovelock) holds that the earth is a single unified organism.

Galilee/Judaea Northern/southern regions of ancient Israel.

Gandhi Mohandas (Mahatma, or "great soul," 1869–1948); great spiritual leader who opposed British occupation of India and originated the non-violent resistance tactic of social protest. Assassinated in 1948.

Ganesha Son of Shiva, popular elephant-headed Hindu god who overcomes obstacles and brings good fortune.

Ganja The Rastafarian word for marijuana; it is smoked ritually by some members of the movement.

Gaon A president of the early medieval Jewish academies (plural: geonim).

Gathas Hymns of Zoroaster written in the ancient Gathic dialect; the oldest portion of the Avesta. They take on the quality of scripture.

Gautama The gotra or clan name (surname) of Prince Siddhartha, the founder of Buddhism; Pali: Gotama.

Gayatrimantra The daily Vedic prayer of upper-caste Hindus.

Ge Hong Author of an influential book on Daoist magic, the Bao Pu-zi (Pao P'u-tzu).

Gemara The part of the Talmud, consisting of Haggadah and some Halakah not included in the Mishnah, that is a collection of rabbinical commentaries (c. 200 to 500 C.E.) on the Mishna in order to connect it to the written Torah.

General Council A meeting of bishops recognized as authoritative by the Eastern Orthodox and Roman Catholic churches; the former accepts only the first seven General Councils, the latter a longer list, including the Second Vatican Council.

Gentiles The name given by Jews to people who were not Jews. Saint Paul saw himself as the apostle to the Gentiles.

Geonim In Judaism, the administrators of the two great rabbinic academies in medieval Babylon.

Ghetto An urban area occupied by those rejected by a society, such as quarters for Jews in some European cities.

Ghost Dance Native revival movement among many Native American peoples in the latter part of the nineteenth century.

Giri Important Japanese sense of social obligation and duty.

Gnosis Intuitive knowledge of spiritual realities.

Gnosticism A type of religious phenomenon that is found in the ancient world, especially in the Hellenistic period (300 B.C.E.–200 C.E.), and largely influenced by Platonic and Zoroastinian dualism. The word *gnosticism* is from the Greek word meaning "knowledge" (*gnosis*), but conveys the idea of a secret knowledge or revelation that will free the soul from its imprisonment in the body and this evil world and return it to its heavenly home. Orthodox Judaism and Christianity saw it as a dangerous heresy.

Gobind Singh The tenth and last Sikh guru (c. 1666-1708), who founded the khalsa, and compiled the Dasam Granth.

Goddess In Wicca, the principal deity, manifested as maiden, mother, and crone (old woman). Her power is called upon in Wiccan rituals.

Gohei In Shinto, zigzag paper streamers (sometimes made of hemp) that are waved over a person's head for purification.

Gohonzon A "personal worship object" used by members of Soka Gakkai to help them meditate on the truths of the Lotus Sutra.

Golden Temple Important Sikh gurdwara at Amritsar.

Good Friday Traditional day of Jesus Christ's crucifixion.

Goshala Makkhali Fatalist and atheist onetime companion of Mahavira; later dominated the Ajivaka order.

Gospel Literally, "good news"; the message concerning Christ, the kingdom of God, and salvation; the first four books of the New Testament (Matthew, Mark, Luke, and John) tell the story of Jesus' ministry and are called the Gospels. Also, a literary term for writings that narrate this proclamation as expressed in the life, death, and resurrection of Jesus.

Gothic cathedrals Large Christian churches built beginning around 1200 C.E., initially in France, with pointed arches, tall ceilings, stained glass, elaborate ornamentation, and external flying buttresses.

Granth Scriptures of Sikhism.

Great Awakening Also known as the First Great Awakening, it was an intellectually serious and more feeling-oriented Christian movement in America during the period from 1720 to 1740 than what had been the case just prior to it. It crossed parish, denominational, and colonial lines and paved the way for the American Revolution in that it gave the people of the 13 colonies a sense of being a distinctive American people with their own spiritual concerns, rather than merely transplanted Europeans.

Guanyin (Kuan Yin) Bodhisattva Avalokiteshvara, widely worshiped in China as a god/goddess of great mercy derived from the Indian Avalokita (Kannon in Japan).

gui (kuei) Earthly yin spirits; ill-disposed and unpredictable malevolent spirits in Chinese popular thought.

Gurdwara ("Gateway of the Guru") A Sikh temple, always containing *Adi Granth*, the first volume of Sikh scriptures. Believers remove shoes, bow before the *Adi Granth shrine*, and hear teachings. Vegetarian food and rooms are provided for wayfarers.

Guru In Hinduism, a spiritual teacher or guide who instructs his followers on the path to liberation; the disciple's relation to the guru is generally considered sacred. In Sikhism, a leader of the religion.

Guru Granth Sahib "Sacred Collection," the Sikh sacred scriptures, with the title Guru; another name for the Adi Granth.

Guru Nanak (born c. 1469 C.E.) Founder of the Sikh faith in India.

Gush Emunim ("Block of the Faithful") A radical Jewish Fundamentalist group of several thousand in Israel that began in the 1970's to settle in the Palestinian territories, contrary to the Israeli governments orders. Its Zionist goal is the entire restoration of the ancient biblical Land of Israel.

Hadith Arabic for "speech, news, event": refers to the narratives (or traditions) of what the Prophet Muhammad said, did, or was like when he established the first Muslim community in Medina. After the Qur'an, the major source for determining Sharia.

Hagar Wife of Abraham, mother of Ishmael and ancestress of the Muslims.

Haggadah A Hebrew term referring to an interpretation of the Tanak that is homiletical rather than legal in nature.

Hainuwele Culture hero in Wemale tradition (Ceram Island in Indonesia) from whose body tuberous plants grew.

Halakhah In Hebrew "that by which one walks" or the body of jurisprudence, ethical duties, and ceremonial observances that for Orthodox Judaism is binding as the word of God. The main sources of *halakhah* are the Hebrew Bible, the Talmud, and a large body of *responsa*.

Han Dynasty A period (206 B.C.E.–220 C.E.) in Chinese history, which paralleled the contemporary Roman Empire in cultural sophistication, and during which China became a Confucian state.

Han Fei Third-century B.C.E. Legalist, author of the Han Fei-zi textbook of statecraft (shu) used by Qin emperors.

Han Synthesis A way of thinking about Chinese religion and culture, which combined aspects of Daoism and Confucianism, and which it developed a quasi-theology, quasi-divinity, and quasi-priesthood for Confucianism and Confucius. Confucius was seen as a sort of mystic king, with a true right to rule the inward kingdom of ideas and values upon which the outer realm, administered and educated by the mandarins, was based. The universe was viewed as a web of correspondences, and the Dao and Yang-Yin were central ideas.

Han Yu Precursor of Neo-Confucianism, in 820 C.E., he protested official veneration of Buddhist relics.

Hanifs Believers in one God who predated Muhammad, including Abraham and some pre-Islamic Arabs.

Hanukkah (Chanuka) Minor Jewish holiday. A joyous event commemorating the relighting of the lamps of the holy temple in the year 165 C.E., during the campaign of the Maccabee brothers to drive out the oppressor.

Haran An important ancient city and caravan stop in north-western Mesopotamia. In tradition, Abraham's father settled there with his family and later Abraham left there to go west to Canaan (Gen. 11:31, 12:4).

Hasidim (Chasidim) From the Hebrew *hasid*, meaning "pietist"; a party among the Jews of Palestine who opposed the hellenizing of Judaism in the second century B.C.E. and were the backbone of Jewish resistance. In modern times, associated with an ultra-orthodox Jewish movement whose members refuse to wear modern Western clothing and whose members dress as their ancestors in the ghettos of eastern Europe. Their piety is marked by a mystical joy and intensity.

Hatha yoga The yoga of physical postures. Body postures, diet, and breathing exercises to help build a suitable physical vehicle for spiritual development.

Hebrew Bible Called the "Tanakh," the whole sacred text of Judaism is divided into the Torah (e.g. Exodus), the Prophets (e.g. Isaiah), and the Writings (e.g. Psalms).

Hebrews The ancient name for the Semitic people of Israel traditionally descended from Abraham. "Hebrew" is found earliest in texts about them in Egypt (Gen. 43:32, Ex. 2). After the Babylonian Exile (586 B.C.E.), the name "Jew" was also used.

Hellenists In New Testament usage (Acts), Christian believers of Gentile background, or of Jewish origin but steeped in Greek culture and practice.

Henotheism From the Greek for "one" and "god"; ascribed to Max Müller, who used it to describe that form of religion in which one god is supreme but others exist; in contrast to monotheism, in which only one god exists.

Heretic A member of an established religion whose views are unacceptable to the orthodoxy.

Hermeneutics The art or science concerned with the conditions and methods required to understand the meaning of a written text. In contrast to *exegesis*, hermeneutics broadly concerns itself with the preconditions that make understanding possible. A specific hermeneutics involves the particular preconditions that are necessary to understand a distinctive text, such as a biblical book or a Buddhist *sutra* or teaching. The term has in recent years been extended to include more than written texts and can refer to the principles for interpreting any human action in order to proceed with rigorous philosophical analysis of that action.

Heuristic From the Greek word for discovery; refers to that which stimulates interest in, and furthers investigation of, a topic.

Heyoka "Contrary" wisdom or a person who embodies it, in some Native American spiritual traditions.

Hidden imam In Shi'ism, the last imam (successor to Muhammad) who disappeared into the state of occultation and will return in the future.

Hierophany Proposed by Mircea Eliade to designate any act or manifestation of the sacred; literally means something sacred showing itself to us.

High Holy Days In Judiasm, Rosh Hashana and Yom Kippur.

Hijab In Islam, head coverings worn by women in keeping with the Qur'an's admonition of modest dress.

Hijra Arabic for "emigration"; the emigration of the Prophet Muhammad from Mecca to Medina in 622 C.E. Muslims date their calendar from this event.

Hinayana In Mahayana Buddhist terminology, the label "lesser vehicle," given to the orthodox southern tradition now represented by Theravada; in Tibetan terminology, one of the three vehicles for salvation taught by the Buddha.

Hinduism, major branches Extremely broad variety, such as 1. *Vaishnava*: followers of Vishnu, 2. *Shaiva* followers of Shiva, developed erotic aspect of religion, such as phallic lingam and temple sculptures, 3. *Shakti* and *Tantra*: goddess-oriented traditions involving sexual energy. Some *sadus*, *sannyasins* and *yogins* practice ascetic austerieies, such as reclining on beds of spikes.

Holi Hindu festival dedicated to the god Krishna.

Holocaust Ancient Israelite ritual meaning "all-consuming sacrificial fire," used in modern times to denote the destruction of Jews and others under the Nazis.

Holy Originally meant that which is separate and wholly other; gradually the term took on the sense of moral perfection. The word is used by Rudolf Otto in its original sense to refer to the Wholly Other, the mysterium tremendum.

Holy Communion The rite of consecrating and consuming bread and wine in remembrance of Jesus' Last Supper with his disciples before the crucifixion; the principle service of worship in Roman Catholic, Eastern Orthodox, and some Protestant churches; also called the Eucharist (an ancient and sometimes Anglican term, now often used in ecumenical contexts), Divine Liturgy (Eastern Orthodox), Mass (Roman Catholic), and Lord's Supper (Protestant).

Honen (1133–1212) The founder of Amidism in Japan, known as Jodo-shu or Pure Land sect.

Hopi Native Americans of southwestern North America.

Horned God In Wicca, the male god, associated with the sun.

Horse sacrifice Elaborate, year-long ritual in ancient India; this ritual involved the sacrifice of thousands of animals.

Huang Di Mythical sage ancestor, the "Yellow Emperor," innovator (silk worm culture, etc.)

Huayan (Hua Yen) A Chinese school of Mahayana Buddhism based on the Garland Sutra.

Hui-neng Sixth (and last) patriarch of the meditative Chan (Zen) tradition in China, seventh-eighth century.

Humanist One who adheres to humanism, a movement which has roots in the Renaissance and which centers on the well-being and values of humans here and now, that is, their secular well-being and values as opposed to their spiritual well-being and values.

Hun The shen soul, seat of the mind; in afterlife, joining the ancestral spirits.

Husayn Son of 'Ali, killed at Karbalah (680); considered by Shi'ites as a successor to the Prophet Muhammad and a great martyr.

Hutterite Brethren An Anabaptist (meaning "re-baptizer") group originating in the sixteenth century in Switzerland but, due to persecution, found asylum in Moravia in 1529 under the leadership of Jacob Hutter. Later the Hutterites migrated to Canada and the United States. Their communities are called Bruderhofs and they hold property in common and practice pacifism.

 **I Ching**   Ancient Chinese book of divination.

Iblis   In Islam, a name for Satan, who is considered to be the personification of evil and chief of the jinn. He rules over hell until Judgment Day, after having been banished from heaven for his disobedience to God.

Icon   From the Greek *eikon*, meaning "image" or "likeness"; a symbolic sacred image, usually painted on flat wood panels or canvas, that materially embodies a spiritual meaning and power. They are sacramental in that they make present the sacred or the divine and are venerated in Eastern Orthodox Christian churches; used especially for the paintings of Jesus, Mary, and the saints of the Eastern Orthodox Christian Church.

'Id al-Adha   Muslim feast of sacrifice.

'Id al-Fitr   Muslim feast of fast breaking. Celebrates a return to normal life after the prolonged fast of Ramadan.

Id   "Feast" or festival in Islam; the two major festivals are 'Id al-adha (Feast of Sacrifice) during the Hajj month and 'Id al-fitr (Feast of Breaking the Ramadan Fast).

Ihram   State of ritual purity and consecration appropriate for entering the sacred precincts of Mecca on the Hajj (Islamic pilgrimage).

Ijma ("Consensus")   For formulating Muslim law, consensus among the legal scholars is necessary.

Ijtihad In Islam   The creative original interpretation of the Qur'an as opposed to strict adherance to traditional interpretations. Independent legal reasoning in Islam; one who does this is a mujtahid.

Um' shallah   Arabic for "if God wills"; a common expression in Islam.

Imam Mahdi ("Guided exemplar")   In Shi'ism an imam divinely appointed to a special messianic role. a leader of prayers and religious life; among Sunnis, the leader of the Islamic community; among Shi'ites, the descendant of 'Ali whom Allah designates as holder of the authority inherent in the line.

Immaculate Conception The doctrine, proclaimed an official dogma of the Roman Catholic Church in 1854, that Mary at her conception was insulated from inheriting original sin-a logically necessary view if sin is defined in Aristotelian terms as a substance.

Immanent Refers to that which is found within, as opposed to transcendent. To speak of God as immanent is to say that God is to be found within, which can mean either within the human soul or within the created order as the inner purpose of the universe.

Impermanence Basic Buddhist doctrine that change is characteristic of everything that arises.

Incarnation Becoming flesh. In Christianity, the doctrine that in Jesus Christ, God (i.e., God the Son, the second person of the Trinity) took on flesh and became a human being. In Hinduism, the avataras or descents of Vishnu or other Hindu gods.

Inclusivism The idea that all religions can be accommodated within one religion.

Indigenous Originating in or pertaining to a particular area or region. Indigenous religions are those native to a geographical area, such as Native American religions.

Indra Vedic storm-warrior god. Aryan god of thunder, rain, and the ruler of heaven.

Indulgences Certificates issued by the pope, the effect of which is to transfer to the penitent some of the grace or merit attained by Christ and the saints and "stored" by the Catholic Church. The perceived abuse of the issuances of indulgences by the pope was one of the main causes of the Protestant Reformation.

Indus Valley Civilization A sophisticated urban culture that flourished along the banks of the Indus River in South Asia, from about 2500 to 1500 B.C.E.

Infidel The Muslim and Christian term for "nonbeliever," which each tradition often applies to the other.

Initiation A process, often arduous, through which a person passes, usually in a traditional programmatic way, to acquire spiritual power and social status within a community, whether as adult member or as shaman.

Inquisition   The use of force and terror to eliminate heresies and non-believers in the Christian Church starting in the thirteenth century.

Institutes of the Christian Religion, The   John Calvin's statement of Christian theology that became a classic for Protestant theology.

International Society for Krishna Consciousness   New religious movement, founded by Swami Bhaktivedanta Prabhupada (1896–1977), Drawing on traditional Hindu practices of worshiping Krishna as the supreme manifestation the divine; known as ISKCON, this movement has drawn many Westerners as devotees.

Ise Shrine   Shrine of Amaterasu, the Japanese Sun Kami.

Ishmael   Son of Abraham and Hagar, ancestor of the Muslims.

Islam   "Submission" in Arabic; name of the religion.

Islam, major branches.   1. *Sunni*: leaders chosen by consensus of community, 2. *Shi'a*: leaders supposed to be descendants of Muhammed, 3. *Sufi*: mystics, such Medlevi Order of whirling dervishes.

Ismailis or "Seveners"   A minority within Shi`a who differ from the "Twelvers" on the identity of the seventh Imam, who, they believe, is the last and hidden one. Ismailism has incorporated many esoteric elements into its beliefs.

Isnad   The chain of transmitters for a particular hadith in Islam.

Israelites   Descendants of Jacob. For a time after King David, it meant only the people of the northern kingdom. Later, by Roman times, it meant all Jews. Today it also implies citizens of the land of Israel.

Izanagi and Izanami   The pair of kami who created the world, according to Japanese mythology.

Izumo   North coastal site of an ancient shrine dedicated to kami, descended from Susa-no-wo.

Jade Emperor Supreme god in Chinese popular religion.

Jainism Indian religion founded by Mahavira that rejects Brahmanic caste and sacrifice, and stresses non-violence ("ahimsa").

Jap Ji The first morning prayer of Sikhs, prayer attributed to Nanak, used in daily devotional rites.

Jataka "Birth story," folk versions of the exemplary lives of animals, demons, and humans, each represnted as a previous life as the Buddha or some other prominent figure in Buddhism.

jati "Birth"; one's caste or closed social group as determined by birth in India.

Jehovah A name for God in Jewish and Christian tradition.

Jehovah's Witnesses Christian movement arising in America, teaching strict literal understanding of biblical ideas and holding firmly to distinctive views such as pacifism, refusal to accept blood transfusions, etc.

Jen Humanity, benevolence—the central Confucian virtue.

Jesus (Aramaic: "Yeshu") The central figure of Christianity; the "Christ," messiah, or savior sent from God as a prophet to teach a new way in Israel. He taught a radical ethic of compassion and alliance with the outcasts that led to his crucifixion and, as Christians believe, his resurrection.

Jethro The Midianite priest whose daugher Zipporah married Moses.

Jewish Temple, First, Second The First great central Temple of the Hebrew people was built in Jerusalem by Solomon during the tenth century B.C.E. (I Kings 6–8). It was a stone rectangle with an interior of cedar and cypress, a front courtyard altar, and an inner "Holy of Holies" room containing the Ark of the Covenant. It was looted and destroyed during the Babylonian conquest in 586 B.C.E.. The much larger Second Temple was built about 520–515 B.C.E., after the period of Babylonian captivity, as described in the biblical books of Ezra and Nehemiah. It lasted until 70 C.E., when the Romans looted and destroyed it and all of Israel. The people were forced to migrate in the "diaspora," as far as Spain and Eastern Europe.

Jiao Important festival in religious Daoism, the Rite of Cosmic Renewal.

Jihad Arabic for "struggle, exertion," referring to the obligation of all Muslims to struggle against error and idolatry, against the inner forces that prevent God-realization and the outer barriers to establishment of the divine order. The "greater" jihad is the individual's personal struggle; the "lesser" jihad is the struggle of the Muslim community to defend itself against those who would destroy the faith.

Jina "Conqueror," Jain idea of one who has reached total liberation; title of one who conquers the desires, binding souls to the world of matter.

Jinn Spiritual creatures recognized in pre-Islamic Arabia. Some could be friendly; others were hostile and demonic.

Jiva In Hinduism, the physical/psychological/social karmic self in Jainism, the life monad, finite and permanent, recipient of karmic effects; the soul. Soul and matter in Jain philosophy. (contrasted with ajiva).

Jizo Popular Buddhist divinity in Japan known as the savior of the dead and helper of dead children.

Jnana Yoga "Knowledge yoga" The use of intellectual effort as a yogic technique. The Hindu discipline of seeking spiritual knowledge and liberation through meditation. Presented in the Bhagavad Gita and other texts.

Jnana-marga Literally "way of knowledge"; salvation is achieved by studying the philosophical implications of Indian sacred writings.

Jodo-shinshu "True Pure Land" Buddhism, a denomination founded by Shinran (1173–1262), the "Martin Luther of Japan."

Jodo-shu "Pure Land" Buddhism, a denomination founded by Honen in Japan (1133–1212).

Judaism, branches 1. *Orthodox:* strict adherence to Torah laws, such as not allowing women rabbis. 2. *Conservative:* Moderate tradition acknowledging importance of Torah laws but allowing some modifications for new conditions, such as women rabbis. 3. *Reform:* Liberal openness to new ideas such as women rabbis and local language in services. Others also.

Judaizers   Christians of Jewish background who held that observance of the Law (circumcision, dietary laws, etc.) should be required of all converts.

Judas   One of Jesus's twelve disciples who betrayed him to the authorities.

Judgment Day   The day on which God will judge all according to their deeds.

Jun-zi   The (morally) superior man, who, as the Confucian ideal suggests, is a man at once a scholar, a selfless servant of society, and a gentleman steeped in courtesy and tradition; as an official and family head, he continually puts philosophy into practice.

Just war   The teaching found in the religions that originated in the Middle East that wars are just if they meet certain criteria (such as being declared by legitimate authorities, and minimizing civilian casualties).

Justification by faith   The Christian teaching that humans receive redemption from sin through trust in what God has done in Jesus Christ, not by any merit of their own.

Ka'bah The cube-shaped stone shrine in the Great Mosque at Mecca, focal point of prayer and pilgrimage for Muslims. It symbolizes the center of the world and is visited by Muslims on the hajj.

Kabbalah "Tradition," especially the medieval mystical Jewish tradition.

Kabir A poet (1440–1518), an important predecessor of Guru Nanak, founder of Sikhism.

Kaddish Jewish public prayer that is characterized by the praise and glorification of God, and by hope in the establishment of God's kingdom on earth; also used as a mourner's prayer, it is recited at the graveside of close relatives and in the synagogue.

Kafir An unbeliever, in Islamic terms.

Kali ("Black mother") Hindu Goddess of death and destruction whose dance shakes the earth to its core; typically has four arms, necklaces of skulls, and a protruding tongue.

Kali Yuga In Hindu world cycles, an age of chaos and selfishness, including the one in which we are now living.

Kalpa A cosmic era; in Jainism, a "spoke" on the wheel of cyclical enhancement and deterioration; a unit in the cycle of periodic dissolutions and reconstitutions of all things.

Kalpa Sutra A segment of the Shvetambara canon of scripture recounting the lives of the Jinas.

Kama pleasure One of the four goals, especially appropriate to the householder stage of life. As Kama, the love god, he shoots flower arrows.

Kamakura Reformation The Kamakura was a period in Japanese history (1185–1333), during which several new forms of Buddhism emerged (e.g., Pureland, Nichiren, and Zen), all of which represented a radical Buddhist simplification in which there was to be a simple and sure key to salvation, as dependable on the battlefield as in the monastic temple. Parallels can be drawn to the Protestant Reformation in Europe.

Kama-sutra A Hindu text, which describes the ways to sensuous and sexual pleasure.

Kami The Shinto word for that invisible sacred quality that evokes wonder and awe in us, and also for the spirits or divinities in Shinto, including mythological beings, powerful and awesome aspects of nature, and important humans. Some scholars see this word as equivalent to mana, but no exact English translation has been achieved.

kami-dana Literally, "god shelf"; the center of domestic Shinto in a Japanese home. A shelf, or altar,where sacred objects are kept and daily prayers are said.

Kannagara Harmony with the way of the kami in Shinto.

Kannon Bodhisattva Avalokiteshvara Popular goddess of mercy in Japan (Guanyin in China).

Karah parshad Sacred food used in the Sikh worship assembly.

Karaites Medieval Jewish group that denied the authority of the Talmud and tried to live exclusively by the rules of the Hebrew bible.

Karma Sanskrit for "action"; the law that explains human behavior as the chain of causes and effects resulting from desire. According to the religions that originated in South Asia, karma binds us to the cycle of rebirth. In Pali, written as kamma. In Jainism, the idea of subtle form of matter that clings to the soul because of the soul's passion and desire, causing rebirths.

Karma Activity Cosmic and personal cause and effect by which one's thoughts and deeds determine what happens to on, whether good or bad, including one's future rebirths. Im moksha, one trancends karma.

Karma-yoga The path of unselfish service in Hinduism. Attaining liberation through selfless work in the world and following one's own dharma.

Karuna In Vajrayana Buddhism, the masculine principle, which represents form, activity, and compassion.

Kashrut Ritual fitness, suitable for use according to Jewish law; applies especially to dietary laws, what foods can and cannot be eaten, and how to prepare them.

Kenosis "Emptying out"; in ritual, the movement of separation or doing away with the old state.

Kenotic   In Russian Orthodox Christianity, belief in the monastic pattern of ascetic poverty combined with service in the world.

Kensho   Sudden enlightenment, in Zen Buddhism.

Ketubah   In Judaism, the marriage contract. It is often an elaborately decorated work of art as well.

Kevala   The supremely perfected state or the highest state of enlightenment, in Jainism.

Khadija   The first wife (d. 619) of the Prophet Muhammad.

Khalsa   "Pure"; the members of the Sikh military fraternity, distinguished by the wearing of the "five k's": kesh, uncut hair; kangha, comb; kach, short pants; kara, steel bracelet; and kirpan, sword. Founded in 1699 by Gobind Singh, the tenth guru.

Kharijites   "Seceders"; strict moralistic sect of early Islam.

Kibbutzim   Agricultural communes in Israel.

Kingdom of God or Kingdom of Heaven   The reign or rule of God, where God's will is done and his power is evident. Jesus said this reign or rule is both present and coming through his ministry.

Kirtan   Devotional singing of hymns from the Guru Granth Sahib in Sikhism.

Kirtana   In Hinduism, devotional group worship through song and dance.

Koan   In Chan or Zen, an enigmatic riddle or saying intended to challenge ordinary rational thought and help one realize one's true nature such as "What is the sound of one hand clapping?"

Kobo Daishi   Originally Kukai (773–835), He was the founder of Shingon Buddhism and wrote a book trying to synthesize Daoism, Confucianism, and Buddhism.

Kojiki Records of Ancient Matters, Earliest writing in Japan, a compilation of stories about the age of the kami and the beginnings of Japan.

Kong Fu-zi Founder of Confucianism (literally "Master Kong"-Latinized as Confucius).

Konkokyo A new Japanese religion.

Kosher Literally, "fit," "proper"; that which is ritually clean or acceptable in Judaism; usually applied to food or food preparation.

Krishna Hindu god prominent in the Bhagavad Gita. Devotees of Vishnu consider Krishna to be an avatar of Vishnu. Originally, an indigenous folk-god, but later one of the principal devotional deities of bhaki in India. His worship is now worldwide.

Kshatriyas The classical warrior class in Hindu society.

Kuan-yin The "Goddess of Mercy" or "Goddess of Compassion" in Pure Land Buddhism in China. Also known as Guanyin, as Kannon in Japan, and as Kwanseum in Korea. Originally this bodhisattva was the male Avalokiteshvara in India.

Kuei Evil spirits recognized in early Chinese religions.

Kufr In Islam, the sin of atheism, of ingratitude to God.

Kuki Great Japanese Buddhist thinker (773–835) and founder of Shingon.

Kundalini In some yogic teaching, coiled power at the base of the spine that can be raised for spiritual growth.

Kusti The sacred cord given to a young Zoroastrian boy or girl at the initiation ritual (Naojote).

Kyoha Shinto "Faith-group," sectarian, or shrine Shinto as distinguished from State Shinto (Jinja Shinto).

Kyoto ("Capital City") Japanese center of numerous Zen monasteries with beautiful gardens.

Lakshmi Goddess of good fortune and prosperity, the favorite wife of Vishnu.

Lama In Tibetan Buddhism, a spiritual teacher.

Langar In Sikh tradition, a free communal meal without caste distinctions.

Laozi (Lao Tzu) Legendary author of the Dao de jing and founder of Daoism (according to tradition, b. 604 B.C.E.).

Last Supper The Christian sacrament of Communion/Eucharist based on the Gospel account of Jesus' meeting for Passover meal with his disciples, sharing bread and wine, just before his capture and crucifixion.

Lectionary A book that contains a table of readings from the Bible to be read in public worship. Particular passages or lessons are apportioned for use on particular days, usually on a two- or three-year cycle.

Legend Story about the past that is popularly taken to be historical and that does have some historical basis but includes elements of the fictitious and even fabulous.

Lent Christian season of penitence in preparation for Easter celebration.

Li The Confucian virtue of "propriety, right form," as expressed in the proper conduct of ritual and right behavior in relationships.

Li Shi-min Seventh-century C.E. Tang emperor, instituted civil service examinations on Daoist texts.

Liberal theology A movement in the nineteenth and early twentieth centuries accepting the findings of evolutionary science and historical-critical study of the Bible and stressing the immanence of God, the Atonement as moral example, the potential for good in human nature, and a social gospel for the constructive reform of society. It holds that the primary message of the Gospels is one of a "view from below," which provides one with the perspective needed to liberate the oppressed.

Liberal Flexible in approach to religious tradition; inclined to see it as metaphorical rather than literal truth. Stresses the importance of adapting the religion's teachings and practices as times change.

Lie-zi   Legendary Daoist of Zhuang-zi's time, known by the third-century C.E. book of Lie-zi.

liminal   In ritual, the state between separation (kenosis) and restoration (plerosis).

Linear   Views of time; depiction of time as having a beginning, middle, and end.

Lingam/yoni   Phallic symbol, often a stone cylinder, representing the great Hindu god Shiva as the male principle, usually ringed by the female yoni, together symbolizing the reproductive energy of life.

"Little tradition"   The name given to beliefs, practices, and social institutions that are outside of the official orthodoxy of a religion. Although historically women have played only minor roles in the authoritative institutions of the various world religions, they often played a great role in the "little traditions" that often emerged alongside the official tradition.

Liturgy   Order of prayer, scripture reading, hymns, and exhortations followed in a worship service.

Logical positivism   The view that philosophy has no method independent of that of science and that philosophy's only task is logical analysis. According to the principle of verifiability, which was defended by logical positivists as a way of distinguishing meaningful statements from nonsense, a statement is meaningful if and only if it is analytic or can be verified empirically.

Logos   In Greek, translated as "word," "speech," "discourse," or "reason"; used by the Stoics to refer to the divine Reason or God. The Jewish writer Philo identified the creative, divine word of the Hebrew scriptures with the logos of the Stoics. In the Gospel of John and in the early Church, it was identified with the Son of the Christian Trinity.

Lollards   Wandering preachers; the movement was instituted by John Wycliffe in England during the fourteenth century C.E.

Lot   Son of Abraham's brother Haran, who traveled with him. He later lived in the corrupt city of Sodom, where his family was threatened (Gen. 18–19). Escaping Sodom as God destroyed it, Lot and his wife were told not to look back, but she did, and consequently she was turned into a pillar of salt.

 **Lotus Sutra** A sutra of Indian origin extremely influential in Chinese and Japanese Buddhism, especially Tian tai, Tendai, and Nichiren. It emphasizes simple devotion and the universal grace of the Buddha stressing that the true Buddha is the cosmic Buddha who wants to show compassion for all beings.

Lugbara A people of East Africa.

Lun Yu The Analects, a collection of the sayings of Confucius.

Lutheran The Reformation teaching and practice of Martin Luther, who emphasized the sole authority of scripture and "justification by faith," the receiving of God's saving grace through inward faith, as cornerstones of Christianity; the term is used more in America than in Europe.

Maat   Ideal of justice and order in ancient Egypt.

Maccabean   Name given to the patriotic Jewish warriors in the second century B.C.E., named after their leader, Judas Maccabeus, who resisted pagan (Greek) practices. The story is told in I Maccabees and is celebrated in the Jewish Festival of Hanukkah. Their dynasty, the Hasmoneans, headed an independent Jewish state until the Romans came in 63 B.C.E.

Madhva   Thirteenth-century philosopher who further modified Ramanuja's qualified nondualism into a fully dualistic (dvaita) system.

Madhyamika   The "middle" (between being and nonbeing) doctrine of Nagarjuna, allowing a conditional distinction between samsara and Nirvana, but asserting that in perfected wisdom all dharmas are empty.

Magi   Order of priests or seers in ancient Persia and the Hellenistic world versed in astrology and magic.

Magic   The manipulation of other beings through spells, incantations, or other means; in Wicca, the focusing of the five senses to effect change, always positively.

Magisterium   The teaching jurisdiction of the Catholic Church; it bestows the authority to teach doctrine.

Mahabharata   A long Hindu epic that includes the Bhagavad-Gita.

Mahaprajapati   The Buddha's aunt and foster mother. She asked the Buddha to permit herself and 500 women to join the Buddha as his followers. When he finally agreed, the order of Buddhist nuns was created.

Mahavairochana   The great sun Buddha.

Mahavira   The twenty-fourth and last Jina of the present world half-cycle, who according to Jain tradition lived from 599 to 527 B.C.E.

Mahayana   The "greater vehicle" in Buddhism, the more liberal and mystical Northern School, which stressed the virtue of altruistic compassion rather than intellectual efforts at individual salvation. So named because of the belief that its teachings provide a "large vehicle" to carry people across the river of rebirth to liberation.

Mahdi   Arabic for "the guided one"; in Islam in general, a descendant of the Prophet Muhammad who will restore justice on earth. In Shi'ite Islam, a messianic imam who will appear in order to end corruption.

Maimonides   Great medieval Jewish philosopher (1135–1204 C.E.).

Maitreya   The next Buddha to appear, who will lead many followers to liberation.

Malleus Malificarum   A book published by two Dominican monks in 1486; it sets out the methods for discovering witches and obtaining confessions from them, usually through horrific tortures.

Mana   Polynesian term for the impersonal supernatural force to which certain primal peoples attribute good or evil fortune or magical power.

Mandala   A symmetrical diagram, circular or square; symbolic representation of the the sacred cosmos, reality, or those energies depicted as deities, demons, Bodhisattvas, and the Buddha. Used in meditation practices in some schools of Buddhism.

Mandarins   The quasi-priesthood of Confucianism; a class of scholar/bureaucrats who administered and educated society (Also known as the Ru).

Mandate of Heaven   In Chinese religion, the expression of Tian's moral will, especially in granting prosperity to virtuous rulers and cutting short evil ones. The right to rule is, withdrawn when a leader or regime fails to fulfill the responsibility to maintain harmony and rule justly.

Mantra   A sacred sound of one syllable or more. In Hinduism, repeated during meditation in order to empty the mind in preparation for liberation; in Buddhism, expresses the essence of some transcendental power or being such as the Buddha or Bodhisattva. The most famous is the syllable *OM*. Plural: mantram.

Manu   Name of a mythic father of the human race; the Code of Manu (ca. 200 B.C.E.–200 C.E.) set out Brahmanic law.

Manushi Buddhas   Buddhas who, like Gautama, have taken form as human beings, taught the liberating Dharma, and gone on to Nirvana.

Manyoshu "Collection of Myriad Leaves," an anthology of over four thousand short poems (ca. 650 to 750 C.E.) written by individuals from virtually every class of society.

Mao Zedong (1893–1976) The founder and the first chairman of of the People's Republic of China. Nearly deified by many, historians have likened his leadership and following to that of a religious cult. His charismatic leadership and ideas led to the Great Cultural Revolution. Transliteration also spelled Mao Tse-Tung.

Mappo In Buddhism, the last age, when doctrine and morality will deteriorate so much that one can be saved only by faith, if at all; concept of considerable importance during the Kamakura Reformation.

Marcionism Views attributed to Marcion of Sinope (second century C.E.), who accepted Gnostic-Docetic ideas and urged that Christians should repudiate the Old Testament and its matter-contaminated deity; he proposed a canon of edited Gospels and ten Letters of Paul.

Marduk God of ancient Babylon city-state.

Marga A path or way as in Karma Marga (the Way of Works), Jnana Marga, and Bhakti Marga.

Marranos Spanish Jews who were outwardly Christianized but who secretly continued Jewish tradition.

Martyr From Greek for "witness," one who dies for a faith or cause.

Mary, mother of Jesus The mother of Jesus from Nazareth. Believed to be a virgin at Jesus' birth, thus guaranteeing that Jesus' father was God. Highly esteemed by Roman Catholics.

Masada Mountain fortress near the Dead Sea where Jewish Zealots made a last stand against the Romans.

Masochism Broadly associated with the feeling of pleasure that a person derives from being abused or dominated by another person or institution.

Mass (Latin *missa:* "Go forth") The central Roman Catholic (and some Protestant) ritual, always including Eucharist, of celebration and worship of God, including song, prayer, and scripture reading.

Master or mistress of animals Divine being, often a prototype of the herd of animals, who protects the herd and also provides boons for humans.

Materialism The tendency to consider material possessions and comforts more important than spiritual matters, or the philosophical position that nothing exists except matter and that there are no supernatural dimensions to life.

Matsuri Shinto shrine festival.

Matteo Ricci First Jesuit missionary to China (1552–1610).

Maya "Illusion"; the concept in Hinduism that reality as experienced is not true reality and constitutes a veil that must be penetrated; the attractive but illusory physical world. In the Upanishads, all that is not Brahman all perceptions, all individuality.

Mazu Widely worshiped goddess of Chinese seafarers; known as the Queen of Heaven.

Mecca The Arabian city at the center of the Muslim world. When Muslims pray, they prostrate themselves in the direction of Mecca.

Medicine man Native American religious functionary whose primary task is to heal by religious means.

Medina The Arabian city to which the Prophet Muhammad emigrated in 622 C.E., and where he established the first Muslim community.

Meditation Focused, disciplined concentration intended to lead to experience of the sacred.

Megalith Large stone monument apparently built for religious purposes, such as Stonehenge and Easter Island Statues.

Megalithiam The practice in many late Neolithic cultures around the work of erecting monuments of large upright stones, sometimes oriented toward the seasonal rising of astronomical bodies. Often they mark burial and ritual sites, but in some cases their purpose is not fully understood. One of the best-known examples is Stonehenge in England.

Meiji Restoration Restoration of imperial rule in Japan in 1868.

Mencius Next to Confucius himself, the greatest philosopher of Confucianism (372–289 B.C.E.), who held that human nature is basically good and is only impeded by an evil social environment.

Mendelssohn, Moses Jewish Enlightenment thinker (1729–1786).

Mendicant A beggar; in many religions, such as Christianity and Buddhism, the act of begging for alms is (or was) a high form of the spiritual life and discipline.

Menorah In Judaism, the eight-branch candelabra which holds candles that are lit successively during the eight-day Hanuka celebration.

Mesopotamia ("Land between two rivers") The ancient settled region between and around the Tigris and Euphrates rivers, east of the Mediterranean Sea, once Babylonia, now Iraq.

Messiah Hebrew for "anointed one"; the hoped-for descendant of King David who will appear to restore Israel to glory. Christians identified the messiah (Greek christos) with Jesus.

Metaphysics The philosophical inquiry into the nature of ultimate reality. The term can also refer to the analysis of fundamental principles used in philosophical analysis.

Metta In Buddhist terminology, loving-kindness.

Middle Way Buddhist principle of avoiding attachment to extremes, such as materialistic pleasure or extreme self-denial.

Midian A son of Abraham and his concubine Keturah (Gen. 25), and his descendants, who became the migrant tribes of desert herders, known best for their hospitality to Moses in the Sinai region after he escaped slavery in Egypt.

Midrash Interpretation of the Tanak in a verse-by-verse commentary. May be haggadic or halakhic.

Mihrab The niche in a Muslim mosque indicating the direction of Mecca, so believers can bow in that direction.

Mikva A deep bath for ritual cleansing in Judaism.

Millenarianism   First appears in the New Testament Book of Revelation in connection with the final struggle between God and Satan and the second coming of Christ in the immediate future, all of which precede the millennium-the 1,000-year reign of the Messiah. Used, however, to describe a large variety of Christian and non-Christian apocalyptic movements that expect a redeemer to inaugurate a Utopian Age. Often used interchangeably with "messianism" or "messianic movements."

Miluo   The Buddha of the future, depicted in China as the fat, laughing Buddha surrounded by playing children.

Mina   A location east of Mecca where pilgrims go to spend a night, throw seven pebbles at a pillar symbolizing Satan (*Jamrat al-Aqaba*), and perform an animal sacrifice.

Minaret   The tall tower beside many Muslim mosques from which the muezzin calls out the believers to prayer.

Minbar   In a Muslim mosque, the seat atop a short flight of steps from which the imam delivers sermons during the Friday prayer.

Ming Dynasty   A period in Chinese history of commercial and literary prosperity; known for its invention and perfection of the art of porcelain-making, as well as the construction of the Imperial Palace in Peking, now Beijing (1368–1644 C.E.).

Minyan   The quorum of ten adult males required for Jewish communal worship.

Mishnah   From the Hebrew, meaning "to repeat, or teaching, tradition, study"; the collection of oral Jewish law, in contrast to the written Law, or Torah, that was compiled by Rabbi Judah Ha-Nasi, circa 200 C.E. Six divisions of the Mishnah cover laws of agriculture, festivals, women, marriage, and so forth. Together with the Gemara, commentary on the Mishnah, it forms the bases of the Talmud.

Misogi   The Shinto waterfall purification ritual.

Mitakuye oyasin   Lakota for "all my relations." Used in Lakota rituals to emphasize that they are "for everyone and everything."

Mithra (Mithras)   Pre-Zoroastrian Aryan deity who appears in Hindu Vedic literature as Mitra, in Zoroastrianism as the judge of the dead, a god of light, protector of the pasture and as the leading figure in a Roman mystery religion.

Mitzvot Jewish term for commandments; acts in obedience to God's will

Moghul Empire (Mughal Empire) Muslim rule of portions of India between the sixteenth and eighteenth centuries C.E.

Moira What is allotted, fate in Greek thought.

Mojtahed (Irani) "Judge," an expert scholar in the application of reasoning (ijtihad) to interpret Islamic law (Arabic: mujtahid).

Moksha From Sanskrit, meaning "liberation" in Hinduism; liberation from the round of birth, death, and rebirth. Various classical schools of Hinduism define in different ways what constitutes liberation and the methods of achieving it.

Mollah (Irani) A Muslim local cleric: tutor and administrator of communal activity centered at a mosque (Arabic: mawla).

Monasticism A way of life withdrawn from ordinary pursuits and dedicated to the sacred. The way of life of the monk or nun, a person who characteristically is celibate (unmarried for religious reasons), has no or few personal possessions, and lives a regulated life of prayer, work, study, and service in a community of such persons. The residence may be called a monastery or convent and is under a superior (abbot, prior, father superior, mother superior) to whom the others owe obedience. Distinctive garb is usually worn by monastics.

Mondo "Question-answer," Zen training material in dialogue format.

Monism From the Greek, meaning "one"; applied to those doctrines that teach that only one being exists, as differentiated from pantheism, which teaches that all beings are divine or that God is in everything. The view that all reality is one, typically emphasizing spiritual unity. Especially associated with Indian nondualism or Advaita Vedanta.

Monotheism The doctrine that there is only one transcendent Creator God as opposed to belief in many gods. Judaism, Islam, and Christianity are examples of monotheistic religions.

Moral evil Suffering in the world caused by human perversity, in contrast to that caused by the processes of nature.

Mores A term used by anthropologists to refer to the customs or folkways of a people that have taken on moral significance and have the force of law.

Mormonism New religious movement founded in America by Joseph Smith (1805–1844) on the basis of the Book of Mormon, also known as the Church of Jesus Christ of Latter-Day Saints, with headquarters in Utah. The name "Mormon" is used to refer to members of the LDS Church.

Moroni The son of Mormon, who, as an angel, appeared to Joseph Smith and directed him to the golden tablets on which the Book of Mormon was inscribed.

Moses Leader of Israel in the Exodus from Egypt and the founding of the covenant on Mt. Sinai.

Mosque A Muslim building for prayer. Some are domed, some have open courtyards. Usually have one to four tall, narrow minaret towers.

Mother Teresa (1910–1997) A Roman Catholic nun born in Albania. Drawn to serve the ill and dying in the streets of Calcutta, she formed the Missionaries of Charity, who take dying people off the streets and nurse them at their Home for Dying Destitutes. She was awarded the Nobel Prize in 1978.

Motoori Norinaga Leading scholar (1730–1801) of the National Learning movement that advocated the restoration of Shinto as Japan's central religion.

Mount Arafat The hill outside of Mecca where Muhammad gave his farewell sermon in that city and where the faithful on pilgrimage stand throughout the afternoon.

Mount Sinai (also called Horeb) The most important of several Hebrew holy mountains whose actual location is unknown, where in tradition Moses saw the Burning Bush (Ex. 3) and later received the Ten Commandments (Ex. 19–20).

Mo-zi (ca. 468–390 B.C.E.) Proletarian advocate of universal love and a heaven-sanctioned utilitarian society.

Mu'tazilites School in the classical period of Islam that accepted reason as a primary criterion for establishing beliefs.

Mudra A hand position, sign, token, or symbolic posture in Hinduism and Buddhism; each *mudra* signifies a mood, virtue, or spiritual quality.

Muezzin One who calls the faithful to prayer at the proper times from the minaret of the mosque.

Muhammed (570–632 C.E.) Born in Mecca, Arabia, he was an illiterate orphan who had visionary experiences. He married Khadijah, who had employed him on her camel caravans, where he met Jews and Christians. He retreated frequently to Mount Hira, where he felt the presence of the divine instructing him to write the Qur'an, the sacred text of Islam. He taught a strong monotheism of Allah in the Abrahamitic tradition, opposed local polytheists, and had to fight to survive and establish Islam.

Muharram The Shi`ite festival which commemorates the death of Husain, the third Imam and the most worthy and tragic of all.

Mujahid In Islam, a selfless fighter in the path of Allah.

Muktad Zoroastrian All Soul's Day honoring departed ancestors.

Mulla Persian word for learned Muslim teacher and expounder of the law.

Muni A Jain monk.

Murshid A spiritual teacher, in esoteric Islam.

Muslim Literally, "submitter" (one who submits to the will of God); one becomes a Muslim by utterance of the Shahadah: "There is no God but God, and Muhammad is the messenger of God."

Mut'a A temporary marriage requiring at least an oral contract for compensation and a fixed, but renewable, termination.

Mysterium tremendum et fascinans The mystery which both terrifies and attracts; Rudolf Otto's term for the experience of the sacred.

Mystery That which is beyond human understanding. In contrast to a problem, which can be solved by an increase in knowledge, no amount of additional knowledge can dispel a mystery. Used by Gabriel Marcel to discuss that which finite human beings cannot understand.

Mystery religions Associated especially with the secret religious cults of ancient Greece and Rome that practiced rites of initiation involving purification, the revealing of secret teachings and symbols, and a sacramental meal of communion with a person's fellows and with the divinity. The chief Greek cults were the Eleusinian and Orphic mysteries.

Mystical Aspects of religious traditions which focus on the appearance of the sacred to persons achieving a certain "enlightened" state of mind.

Mysticism An experience is mystical if it is characterized by a sense of unity and oneness with the divine. One variation is union mysticism, characterized by loss of individuality and transportation beyond time and space into an experience that is ineffable. Another variation is communion mysticism, in which the individual experiences a sense of unity of purpose and communion with the divine but does not lose a sense of individuality. Communion mysticism is more characteristic of both Jewish and Christian mystical experiences than is union mysticism, although the latter does have its representatives within both traditions.

Myth A story that expresses in narrative form something of the fundamental worldview of a society. Also a story about the sacred, which is foundational, creating the basic patterns of life for people who accept the story as true for them. A cosmogonic myth tells the story of the ordering of reality, and an eschatological myth tells the story of the end of the current age and the beginning of a new one.

Nabi One called to speak for God, a prophet.

Naga A snake, worshipped in Hinduism.

Nagarjuna Ca. 150–250 C.E. Author of the Madhyamika-karikas, best-known text of the Madhyamika or "middle doctrine" school.

Nam The holy Name of God reverberating throughout all of Creation, as repeated by Sikhs.

Nam-Marg "The Path of the Name," Sikh self-reference to distinguish it from Hindu paths: "Bhakti Marga," and so on.

Nanak Founder (1469–1539) of Sikhism and the first guru.

Naojote The ritual of initiation for young Zoroastrian boys and girls, in which they are invested with the sacred shirt and sacred cord (kusti).

Natural evil The suffering in the world due to the processes of nature, in contrast with suffering caused by human perversity. Floods, hurricanes, earthquakes, and disease are examples of natural evil.

Natural law The universally valid principles of conduct known by reason alone and therefore accessible to all people, as opposed to the positive law of a state or society. Originating in ancient Greek philosophy, natural law theories were used by philosophers of the Middle Ages as another proof of the existence of God, who was thought to be the author of the natural law.

Natural theology That which can be known about God purely by the power of human reason unaided by revelation. Natural theology claims to be able to provide proofs of God's existence either completely a priori, and therefore independent of the senses, or a posteriori, that is, based on certain facts about the natural order.

Navajo Native American people of southwestern North America.

Ndembu People living in Zambia in Central Africa.

Neanderthal A type of prehistoric man from the middle Paleolithi age, whose remains were found in a cave in the Neanderthal Valley near Dusseldorf, Germany with clear archaeological evidence of religious activities.

Nembutsu Contraction of "Namu Amida Butsu" (Hail, Amida Buddha), mantra of the Japanese Jodo sect.

Neo-Confucianism Revival of Confucian thought in the eleventh century C.E., with emphasis on the underlying principle of all things.

Neolithic The New Stone Age, when planting was discovered and villages and cities founded, and when most tools, weapons, and the like were constructed from stone. that began about 8000–7000 B.C.E. in the Middle East and about 4000–3000 B.C.E. in Europe. It was followed by the Bronze Age.

Neo-orthodoxy Modern Protestant theological movement reasserting orthodox tradition about human sinfulness and divine grace.

Neo-Pagans Broad new religious movement emphasizing nature spirituality on the basis of pre-Christian traditions about gods, goddesses, and sacred nature, including various groups such as druids, witches, goddess-worshipers, and more.

Nestorianism The doctrine of Nestorius of Constantinople (fifth century), still held in some Eastern Churches, that Christ had two distinct "natures," human and divine, and that the Virgin Mary should not be called Mother of God (theotokos).

New Age Movement Broad term sometimes used to identify the religious subculture that emphasizes personal transformation and growth through spiritual techniques like channeling, planetary consciousness, shamanism, astrology, use of crystals, and much more.

New Religions in Japan Term used for new religious movements, often drawing on and combining aspects of Buddhism, Shinto, and folk religion.

Ngaju Dayak Agricultural people living in Kalimantan, Indonesia.

Nicene Creed The standard doctrine of Christianity; written at the Council of Nicaea.

Nichiren A Japanese Buddhist reformer (1222–1282 C.E.) and the sect named after him, which incorporates aspects of Buddhism and Shintoism, the indigenous national religion of Japan. Nichiren believed true Buddhism was found in the *Lotus Sutra* and that other forms of Buddhism were in error. A uniquely militant and zealous expression of Buddhism.

Niddah   In Judaism, the rules regarding menstruation.

Nihilism   In ethics the view that there are no principles of morality. The term can also refer to a situation in which there is a complete breakdown of all previous ethical systems and the collapse of moral principles.

Nihongi (Nihon Shoki)   "Chronicles of Japan," an extension (to 697 C.E.) and expansion of the materials of the Kojiki; written in Chinese, compiled shortly after the Kojiki and containing stories about the kami and early emperors.

Niiname-sai   National Japanese festival of the harvest.

Ninety-five Theses   The Ninety-five points of controversy about Roman Catholic doctrine that Martin Luther, according to tradition, nailed to the cathedral door in Wittenberg, Germany in 1517. Beginning of Protestant Reformation.

Ninigi   Grandson of Amaterasu, sent to earth to begin kami rule on earth, ancestor of first legendary Japanese emperor.

Nirgrantha   Literally, "unclothed one"; an ascetic.

Nirmanakaya   The expression of the Buddha-nature as ordinary, "waking" reality.

Nirvana   Literally, "blowing out"; cessation of consciousness.Unconditioned reality, experienced without form or limit when all attachments have been negated and the fires of craving blown out; the ultimate Buddhist goal.

Niyati   Mechanistically determined fate or destiny.

No Ruz   Zoroastrian festival celebrating the New Year.

No-action (Wuwei)   Basic Daoist principle of not doing anything contrary to the flow of nature.

Noble person   Junzi ideal Confucian goal, a noble person defined by moral character.

Noh   Classical Japanese theater Closely linked to the religious traditions, especially Zen.

Nomads A wandering group of people with no fixed home, who move from place to place in search of food and water.

Nontheistic Perceiving spiritual reality without a personal deity or deities.

Norito Prayer(s) and liturgical formulas used in Shinto ceremonies.

Normative The measure or standard by which other beliefs or practices are to be judged.

No-self (An-atman) The basic Buddhist doctrine that there is no permanent, absolute self.

Numinous Spiritual or supernatural A term coined by Rudolf Otto and derived from the Latin term numen, meaning divine power. It refers to that which is experienced as the "wholly other" or as the mysterium tremendum. Otto also referred to the numinous as the holy.

Nyaya Hindu philosophical system that uses logical analysis to arrive at truth about the world.

Objectivism In ethics the view that there are objective principles that are true or false independent of people's feelings about them. Regarding ethical statements, objectivism holds that such statements have a truth value, that is, they can be true or false. The opposite of subjectivism.

Obon (Ullambana) Festival of the seventh month in Japan welcoming the ancestors.

Occult Involving the mysterious, unseen, supernatural.

Oedipus complex The theory of the psychoanalyst Sigmund Freud that children (particularly boys) have an unconscious tendency to be attached to the parent of the opposite sex and to show hostility toward the other parent. Freud used this theory to explain certain social facts, including religion.

Ogun The most widely worshipped orisa; the Yoruba god of war and iron, with associated powers of both formation and destruction.

Oharai Shinto purification ceremony.

Old Testament Christian designation for the Hebrew scriptures.

Olorun "Owner of the sky"; the Yoruba high god, Lord above all, who dwells in the heavens and is the source of all life.

Olympian gods Powerful gods of ancient Greece thought to rule from Mt. Olympus.

OM In Hinduism, the primordial sound.

Omnipotent From the Latin *omni* ("all") and *potens* ("powerful"), meaning "all-powerful"; traditionally ascribed to God in Western monotheism is his having unlimited power and authority.

Omniscient Having infinite knowledge; knowing all things is traditionally ascribed to God in the Western monotheistic religions.

On-giri Relationship In Japan, the relationship between a benefactor and the recipient of benefaction, which results in the benefactor becoming a parent substitute.

Ontological Derived from the Greek word for being, the term relates to the question of being. The nature of being; the branch of philosophy that investigates the nature, the essential properties, and the relations of being. The ontological argument is an argument for God's existence based solely on an analysis of the concept of the being of God. Ontology is the metaphysical inquiry into the nature of being in general.

Oral Torah Legal teachings that supplement the written Torah (the Hebrew Bible), which appeared first orally among Torah teachers but were committed to writing by the late second or early third century C.E. as the Mishnah, and grew to encompass the whole Talmud.

Ordination (Upasampada) Important Buddhist ritual marking the beginning of life as a monk or nun.

Original Sin The Christian doctrine that human beings are inherently sinners because they are descendants of Adam, who failed to obey God. It was fully developed in the writings of Saint Augustine.

Orisha In African mythology, lesser deities who participated in the creation of the world.

Orthodox Judaism School of Judaism that emphasizes a strict following of the Law as traditionally interpreted.

Orthodox Christains Correct in doctrine; the name of the ancient Christian churches of the East, which recognize the first seven General Councils.

Orthodoxy Indicates the standard for "right belief" set by a particular community.

Orthopraxis Similar to orthodoxy, but refers to "right practice."

Osiris God of the dead in ancient Egypt, important for the afterlife.

Ottoman dynasty Ruling much of the Muslim world from Istanbul from the fifteenth to the twentieth centuries C.E.

Pagan/Paganism   Originally referred to all non-Christian religions of the Roman Empire, and today is used pejoratively to refer to nonmainstream religions. In recent decades, the term has been claimed by those in the Neo-Pagan movement of the United States and Europe to refer to a collection of new religions based on or derived from the pre-Christian folk religion roots of Old Europe, as well as from religions of indigenous peoples around the world.

Pagodas   Religious temples and other religious structures in India, China, and Japan, usually associated with Buddhism, but not necessarily so.

Paijusna   Jain festival beginning eight days before the new year; a time of fasting and meditation.

Paleolithic   The Old Stone Age that began with the appearance of the earliest toolmakers and extended to about 10,000–8000 B.C.E. It is characterized by the making of stone tools and weapons and by hunting and food-gathering.

Palestine   The land of the ancient Philistine people along the southern seacoast of what is now Israel, then the larger area now Israel, called "Palestine" by the Romans.

Pali   The Indian dialect first used for writing down the teachings of the Buddha, which were initially held in memory, and still used today in the Pali Canon of scriptures recognized by the Theravadins.

Pali Canon   The Theravada Buddhist scripture, consisting of the Tripitaka ("three baskets"): the baskets of disciplinary regulations, discourses, and higher philosophy.

Palm Sunday   The Christian holiday the Sunday before Easter, celebrating the Gospel account of Jesus' final entry into Jerusalem riding on a donkey. Palm leaves, laid on the road before him, are used to recall Jesus' welcome.

Panchatantra   Animal fables set in a narrative frame depicting them as lessons in practical wisdom (niti), a contrast to academic Brahmanic learning.

Panexperientalism   A term found in process thought to describe reality as occasions of experience rather than static objects. It is preferred by process philosophers to the comparable term panpsychism.

Pangu   In Chinese tradition, mythic primordial person out of whom the whole universe developed.

Panpsychism   The view that all reality is mental, not physical, in nature. A form of metaphysical idealism.

Panth   In Sikhism, the religious community.

Pantheism   From the Greek, *pan* ("all") and *theos* ("god"); the doctrine that all that exists is God and God is all in all. God and nature are interchangeable terms.

Pantheon   From the Greek, meaning "all the gods"; designates all the gods of a society taken collectively. Derives from the great Pantheon at Rome, a temple built in 27 B.C.E. and dedicated to all the gods.

Parable   A story, usually fictional, in which the thrust of the story is to make a particular point but in which (by comparison with allegory) the characters do *not* "stand" for realities outside the story itself. Parables are the stories by which Jesus taught his disciples about the Kingdom of God.

Paraclete   The entity that Jesus said would come after his death to help the people.

Parinirvan   "Final" or "complete" Nirvana, for example, the Buddha in the last hours of his final departure from the world of phenomena.

Parsis   "Persians," the name for the Zoroastrian community in India.

Parvati   Hindu Goddess, dark-skinned wife of Shiva, typically pictured making love with Shiva or seated with him on Mount Kailasa discussing Hindu philosophies.

Passion story   The climax of each of the four Gospels, telling of the suffering and crucifixion of Jesus.

Passover   The Spring holiday of Judaism that commemorates the freeing of the Hebrew slaves from Egyptian oppression and the Exodus from Egypt of the Hebrews to the promised land. God "passed over" the dwellings of the Hebrews when he smote the first born of the Egyptians.

Pastoralists   Peoples who live by raising herds of cattle or sheep and whose religious ideas are associated especially with their herds.

Patanjali Author of the Yogasutras, the key work in the Yoga school of philosophy.

Path of Action (Karma-marga) Hindu path toward liberation based on acting according to Dharma, without desire for the fruits of action.

Path of Devotion (Bhakti-marga) Hindu path toward liberation based on devotional practices directed toward one's god.

Path of Knowledge (Jnana-marga) Hindu path toward liberation based on knowledge, emphasizing meditation.

Path of Transformation Practice in a religion that changes one from the wrong or inadequate state to the ideal state.

Patriarch A title given the bishop of certain ancient and important cities; in particular, the Patriarch of Constantinople (Istanbul); the senior official of the Eastern Orthodox Church.

Patriarchy Literally, the "rule of the fathers." Term used by feminists and others to denote a society where all of the authority is held by men.

Paul Leading apostle who brought the gospel of Christ to non-Jews and whose letters form part of the New Testament.

Penance Sacrament (of the Roman Catholic, Orthodox, and some Anglican churches) in which the Christian confesses sin and receives absolution; also, an act performed to show sorrow or repentance for sin, and making restitution for ethical impurities in order to be fit to approach the Sacred.

Peng-lai Mythic blessed isle(s), where magic mushrooms confer immortality upon the xian.

Pentateuch The five books of Moses at the beginning of the Hebrew Bible.

Pentecost In Judaism, the "Feast of Weeks," which celebrates the receipt of the Law by Moses on the fifteenth day after the Exodus from Egypt. In Christianity, the celebration on the seventh Sunday after Easter, commemorating the descent of the Holy Spirit on the apostles, also known as Whitsunday.

Pentecostal/Pentecostalist   Related to Pentecost in that it involves emotional and ecstatic practices as evidence of the Holy Spirit.

People of the Book   In Islam, designates religions that have sacred texts, especially Judaism and Christianity.

Petition   To ask or beg favors of the sacred.

Peyote   A small cactus that contains a drug that causes visions or feelings of euphoria when consumed; used as a sacrament in the Native American Church.

Peyote religion   Modern Native American revival movement, called the Native American Church, with ceremonial use of peyote (small hallucinogenic cactus).

Pharaoh   Title of the ancient Egyptian king. Pharaoh Ramsses II (1279–1212 B.C.E.) is thought to be the Pharaoh of the period of Hebrew slavery in Egypt (Exodus).

Pharisees   A party within Judaism, active in the last centuries B.C.E. and first century C.E., composed of lay people dedicated to keeping the commandments of the written and oral Torahs; opposed to the Sadducees. Contemporary Judaism descends from Judaism as understood by the Pharisees.

Phenomenology   An approach to the study of religion which focuses on description of the concrete beliefs and practices of religious people and/or groups.

Philosophy   Humanistic, rational thinking that developed especially in ancient Greece.

Pietism   A Christian reaction to the rationalism of the Enlightenment, emphasizing the experience of God's grace and emotional dedication.

Pilate, Pontius   The Roman Procurator of Judea (c.a. 26–36 C.E.) who traditionally condemned Jesus to crucifixion.

Pilgrimage   A traditional religious journey to view a relic or toward a place and condition of sacredness or healing, common in many religions. In Islam, the great pilgrimage, the *Hajj*, is to Mecca in Saudia Arabia, during the month *Dhul-Hija*. This is one of the five basic duties of Muslims who can afford it. During this a pilgrimage is taken from the Great Mosque to other nearby ritual sites for *wuquf* ("standing"), throwing rocks, sacrificing, and cutting hair. The Hajj brings together Muslims in a huge international community.

Plan of salvation Christian idea of God's design for the salvation of the world foretold through prophets and accomplished through Jesus Christ.

Planters Peoples who cultivate plants for food and have religious ideas associated especially with vegetation and the fertility of the earth.

Plerosis "Filling up"; fulfillment or restoration movement of ritual.

Pluralism The condition, especially apparent in the modern world, in which many different options for belief and lifestyle exist together in the same society.

Po the gui soul Animating bodily organs; in afterlife, dwelling in the earth.

Pogrom An attack against Jews.

Pollution In the Shinto view, anything that hinders life and fertility by causing separation from the kami.

Polysemy A term used in semantics to refer to the feature of a word whereby it has many meanings. Ricoeur uses the term in his discussion of metaphor, which is a kind of polysemy.

Polytheism Recognition and worship of more than one god; conceives of sacred power as being manifested in diverse forms.

Pope Title for the Bishop of Rome; leader of the Roman Catholic Church.

Popular Religion "Religion of the people" as opposed to "official" or authoritative religion.

Positive law Laws enacted by the state or by society to regulate behavior. Such laws are not required to be the same for all people but may reflect societal differences, such as the speed limits in various countries.

Positivism In general a view that rejects the possibility of metaphysics. Auguste Comte suggests that the history of thought has proceeded through three stages the religious, the metaphysical, and the positive. The latter stage is characterized by a rejection of all religious and metaphysical thinking.

Practical form of religious expression A religion's form of worship, prayer, meditation, pilgrimage, and the like. To find a religion's practical expression, start by asking yourself, "What do they do?"

Practical justification The process of giving reasons for the judgments one makes.

Prajna Buddhist term for "wisdom." Prajna-paramita is the wisdom that goes beyond ordinary knowledge to an intuitive experience of the ultimate truth, quiescent complement of upaya (skill in benevolent action).

Prajna-paramita "Wisdom gone to the other shore," "Perfection of Wisdom," or "Wisdom that has gone beyond"; the highest intuitive-enlightenment wisdom in Mahayana; also, the name of a goddess who personifies it.

Prakriti The eternal self-subsisting material world; in Sankhya dualism the coeternal counterpart to purusha, pure consciousness; in advaita Vedanta a product of maya. In Samkhya Hindu philosophy, the cosmic substance.

Pralaya A time of nullity or rest for the universe at the end of a period of dissolution.

Prana In Indian thought, the invisible life-force.

Pranayama Yogic breathing exercises.

Prasad In Indian traditions, blessed food.

Prayer A deliberate attempt on the part of a person to communicate with the sacred; can take different forms.

Predestinarian A person who holds the belief in pre-destination-the doctrine that God, from the beginning, has determined the ultimate destiny of every human being, some to salvation and others to damnation.

Predestination The notion that the ultimate destiny of persons has been eternally established by God; associated with election.

Presbyters Members of a local board of elders of a Christian Protestant sect; refers to lay governance as opposed to governance by ordained priests.

Priest Religious specialist associated with sacramental elements of religious traditions.

Principle Li Neo-Confucian concept of the underlying source of all phenomena.

Process theology A theological view that sees the universe as made of dynamic, interrelated processes, not static, substantial beings. God as conceived of by process thought is not immutable and unchanging but is interdependent with the world and is affected by other entitites of the world. Process theologians tend to identify God with the principle of value, rather than with the principle of reality, and conceive of God as savior of the world rather than as its creator.

Profane "Outside the temple"; that which is ordinary, not sacred the opposite of sacred; ordinary reality, which is yet to be ordered by the sacred.

Prophet Someone commissioned by God to carry a message to a particular people.

Propitiation Act of appeasing, pacifying, or making favorable, often through some form of sacrifice to a deity.

Proposition A proposition is expressed by a sentence that has a truth value, that is, it can be either true or false. The sentence "The book is blue" expresses a proposition. The sentence "Close the door" does not express a proposition. To express a proposition, a statement must have propositional content, which means that it refers to something and predicates a quality of it.

Proselytize Engaging in the effort of persuading or converting a person from one religion or opinion to another; a proselyte is one who has been converted from one religion to another.

Protestantism Christian sects that developed in "protest" to the practices of the Catholic Church during the sixteenth century.

Pu The uncarved block, Daoist symbol of the perfection of the natural state of things.

Pudgala A semipermanent but ultimately perishable "personhood" neither identical with nor separate from the five skandhas.

Puja   In the religions of India, ritual worship of the image of a god by offering food, flowers, music, and prayers.

Punjab   The traditional homeland of the Sikhs, now divided between Pakistan and India.

Puranas   Books deriving from the early Middle Ages, which set out accounts of the folk gods of the indigenous traditions of India. Many of these gods became the devotional gods of bhakti, e.g., Sarasvati and Durga.

Purdah   The practice of secluding women by confining them to the home, thus isolating them from society and limiting their education to domestic vocations.

Pure Land Buddhism   Version of Mahayana Buddhism popular in China and Japan; it teaches that its devotees can be reborn in a paradise, called the "Pure Land of the West," where they can reach enlightenment through faith in the vow of the Buddha Amitabha (Emiduo or Amida) to save all who call upon his name. Called Jodo in Japanese.

Purgatory   In some branches of Christianity, an intermediate after-death state in which sins insufficient to warrant eternal punishment in hell are purged away, so that the soul can eventually enter heaven.

Purification   Ritual preparation for an approach to the sacred; may involve fasting or ablutions.

Purim   The Jewish holiday in February or March that commemorates the story recounted in the Book of Esther: how the Jews were saved from the wicked designs of Haman, chief minister of the Persian king, by Esther the queen and her cousin Mordecai.

Purusha   The Cosmic Spirit, soul of the universe in Hinduism; in Samkhya philosophy, the eternal Self.

Q (Quelle) Designation given to a hypothetical written collection of the sayings of Jesus presumed to have been shared by the compilers of the gospels of Matthew and Luke.

Qi (ch'i) Material force, breath, flowing vital energy, in Chinese traditions.

Qing Ming "Clear and bright" festival; spring festival of visiting and renovating ancestral tombs in China.

Qiyas "Analogy" in legal argumentation and decision making in Islam.

Quakers Religious sect, also known as the "Society of Friends," founded in the 1650s in England by George Fox and others. They were called "Quakers" because they would "quake" when they communed with God inwardly.

Qur'an or Koran Arabic for "recitation"; the collections of revelations received by the Prophet Muhammad from God (Allah) through the angel Gabriel.

Rabbi Hebrew for "my master"; Jewish teachers who interpret the Torah for others and serve as leaders of Jewish communities.

Rabbinic Judaism Designation for Judaism as it developed under the teachers of the oral Torah (Mishnah and Talmud).

Radiance Term used by Thomas Aquinas to refer to a property of beautiful objects whereby they call attention to themselves. Konstantin Kolenda adopts the term to refer to those features of life that bring delight and satisfaction.

Rain Retreat (Vassa) Important three-month time of study and discipline for Theravada Buddhist monks and nuns, when lay people also make offerings and perform service for the monastics.

Raja Originally, this word was applied to Aryan chieftains but later came to describe Indian rulers in general.

Rama The hero of the major Hindu epic, *Ramayana*. A courageous prince, a manifestation of the god Vishnu, Rama was banished to the forest with his wife Sita. She was abducted by the demon Ravana and rescued by Rama after a long battle.

Ramadan Month during which devout Muslims do not eat or drink between sunrise and sunset. The fast celebrates the month in which the Prophet received the Quran.

Ramakrishna Nineteenth-century saint and seer who proclaimed the oneness of all religions; his disciple, Vivekenanda, founded the Vedanta-oriented syncretistic Ramakrishna movement in his honor.

Ramanuja Twelfth-century author of a qualified-nondual (vishisht-advaita) theistic Vedanta school.

Ramayana Epic of the struggles of Rama and his allies in rescuing Sita from the demon Ravana.

Rasul Muhammad's calling in relation to God; means prophet, envoy, messenger, apostle, ambassador, or spokesman.

Rationalism In religion it is the view that truth must be based on reason and not on faith; the opposite of fideism.

Rebirth In the religions of India, belief that after the death of its body the soul takes on another body

Reconstructionism In Judaism, the modern movement that views Judaism as an evolving civilization and interprets religious teaching in light of scientific understanding.

Rectification of names Becoming what one is. In other words, fulfilling one's proper role (e.g., father, son, wife, mandarin) in society to the fullest, motivated by ren (virtue) so that one contributes to the harmonious "dance" of society.

Red Sea A long ocean separating Arabia from Africa. In biblical tradition Pharaoh pursued the escaping Hebrews to the Red Sea, where God separated the waters like a wall on each side, so the Hebrews could cross on dry land. Then the waters rushed back, drowning the pursuing Egyptians (Ex.14). This miracle story shows the power of God to overcome injustice.

Reform In Judaism, the modern movement that stresses loyalty to the essence of the Jewish tradition while adapting Jewish principles to changing times and different cultures.

Reformation Reform movements in the Christian church, especially the reform of the European church through the work of Luther, Calvin, Zwingli, and others.

Reincarnation The religious doctrine of several religions, including Hinduism and Buddhism, that after death human beings are born again in this world or in other worlds as humans or as animals.

Relativism Any view that denies there are objective principles. In ethics it is the view that there are no objective principles of ethics and no values that hold for all people at all times and all places. Instead, it sees values as arising either from human cultures or as legislated by human agreement.

Relics Physical terms (bones, teeth, clothing) associated with a holy person and preserved by believers for their connection with the sacred.

Religious Daoism General term for the variety of Daoist practices related to priests, scriptures, and techniques for prolonging life.

Reliquary   A small box, container, or shrine used to hold or exhibit a religious relic, such as the bones of a saint.

Ren   Confucian term for virtue; a vague but eloquent term suggestive of humanity, love, high principle, and living together in harmony.

Restraints   The Jain vows of nonviolence, not lying, not stealing, refraining from wrong sex, and nonpossession or nonattachment.

Resurrection   The return of the body to life after death, the central traditional phenomenon of Christianity, demonstrating Jesus' divinity and immortality for believers.

Revelation   The disclosure of sacred truth, the manifestation of ultimacy to humans.

Reverend Martin Luther King, Jr., Ph.D. (1929–68)   A Baptist minister from Atlanta, leader of the U.S. Civil Rights movement that nonviolently opposed legalized racial discrimination. King received the Nobel Prize in 1964. He was assassinated in 1968.

Revivalism   A characteristic of certain religious groups, especially within Protestant Christianity, that emphasizes the importance of a personal, emotional conversion and commitment to Christ; effected through "revivals," evangelistic meetings, or even longer periods of religious fervor, in which a religious awakening and conversion of individuals is sought.

Rig-Veda   A collection of over 1,000 Sanskrit hymns, the liturgical handbook of early Aryan hotar priests, the oldest portion of Brahmanic "revealed" (shruti) sacred literature.

Rinzai   School of Zen Buddhism that developed in Japan during the Kamakura period (1185–1333), which taught that the way to enlightenment is through spontaneous insight.

Rishi   A Hindu sage.

Rita   The Vedic term for the cosmic law or order.

Rite of passage   Any of various rituals that mark the passage from one phase in a person's life to another phase (e.g., baptism, circumcision, puberty rites, marriage, death rituals).

Ritual   Activities of many kinds that connect people with sacred realities, including prayer, sacrifice, chanting, pilgrimage, festivals, disciplines of meditation, and much more.

Roman Catholic church   The historic Western Church as it has continued under the leadership of the pope, the bishop of Rome.

Rosary   A string of beads with a crucifix hanging on it, which one uses to count repeated "Hail Marys," or novenas, special sets of prayers on successive days. Also, it refers to the sets of prayers themselves.

Rosh Hashanah   Jewish New Year, first day of Tishri (usually in September); beginning of High Holy Days (which include Yom Kippur).

Rowza (Irani)   A special assembly at a mosque for reading and preaching to intensify grief over Hoseyn's martyrdom and fresh resolve.

Ru jiao   The way of the literati or scholar gentlemen.

Rudra   Mountain god of the north wind, sometimes destroyer, sometimes healer, later worshiped under the name Shiva, "auspicious."

Ryobu Shinto   "Two aspect" Shinto, an amalgamation between Shinto and Buddhism, a syncretized Shinto in which Buddhist bodhisattvas and deities are attended by kami or equated with particular Shinto deities.

Ryobu   Attempted amalgamation between Shinto and Buddhism.

Sabbath The Jewish holy day, beginning at sundown on Friday and ending at sundown on Saturday, commemorating the "day of rest" after the six days of creation.

Sacramental Elements of religious traditions which focus on the appearance of the sacred through the medium of material reality.

Sacraments Certain rites believed to convey God's grace directly and to be generally necessary to Christian salvation. Many Protestant churches celebrate the sacraments of baptism and Holy Communion, while Roman Catholic and Eastern Orthodox churches acknowledge five additional sacraments: confirmation, marriage, holy orders, penance, and extreme unction ("last rites").

Sacred The general term for what is experienced as that which is ultimate, either of a spiritual or secular nature, and which orders reality for believers.

Sacred hoop Symbol of the Oglala Lakota nation; an unbroken circle.

Sacred space Space that is made special by connection with the sacred, providing orientation and rootedness for a people.

Sacred story Master story of a religion, providing identity for the adherents; see myth.

Sacred thread In Hinduism, a cord worn over one shoulder by men who have been initiated into adult upper-caste society.

Sacred time Special time of ritual and festival, when mythic events are made present once more.

Sacrifice From Latin *sacrum facere*, that is, "to make holy"; for example, by dedicating something to the sacred. A ritual in which worshippers present offerings to deities or spirits in exchange for benefits they are seeking.

Sadducees A party in Judaism, composed of priests and their supporters, active from the second century B.C.E. through the first century C.E. They rejected recent oral tradition and reduced Judaism to matters specifically treated in written law.

Sadhu In the Hindu tradition, a wandering holy man who has set aside worldly goals for the sake of the spiritual life; is devoted fully to achieving *moksha*, or liberation.

Safavid Muslim dynasty in Iran, featuring rule by the shahs.

Saga A heroic narrative about either a historical or a legendary figure. Classic sagas were those recorded in Ireland in the twelfth and thirteenth centuries.

Sage Religious specialist associated with mystical traditions.

Sahajdhari Conservative sect in Sikhism.

Saicho Founder (767–822 C.E.) of Tendai Buddhism in Japan.

Saint In Christianity, a person recognized by a church as possessing exceptional holiness.

Salat Required Muslim ritual of prayer five times daily.

Sallakhana Jaina ritual suicide.

Samadhi The final trance state in yogic practice, a foretaste of moksha in which distinctions of subject and object are transcended.

Sambhogakaya The expression of the Buddha-nature as paradisal heavens ruled by radiant Buddhas and bodhisattvas.

Samhitas "Collections" of early Vedic hymns and verses; there are four collections: Rig-Veda, Sama-Veda, Yajur-Veda, and Atharva-Veda.

Samkhya One of the major Hindu philosophical systems, in which human suffering is characterized as stemming from the confusion of Prakriti with Purusha.

Samsara Sequence of change, impermanence, the cycle of rebirth-redeath that afflicts every living being until release (moksha).

Samskaras Hindu "Sacraments" or "rites of passage" performed at definite stages of life, from birth through entry into adulthood.

Samurai The medieval Japanese class of warriors influenced by Zen and Neo-Confucianism.

San Jiao Tang period "Three Religions" school; sought to combine Daoism, Confucianism, and Buddhism.

Sanatana Dharma   The "eternal religion" of Hinduism.

Sanctification   The receipt of the Holy Spirit in a strong, emotional conversion experience.

Sandpainting   Navajo ceremonial art used in healing rituals.

Sangat   A Sikh congregation, in which all are ideally considered equal.

Sangha   In Theravada Buddhism, the monastic community; in Mahayana, the spiritual community of followers of the dharma.

Sanhedrin   The supreme political, religious, and judicial council of leaders for Jews in Israel in Roman times. Called the "Court of 71," a group of priests and Torah scholars who debated Jesus' fate.

Sannyasin   In Hinduism, a person who has renounced the world and its possessions and has become an ascetic, seeking liberation through prayer and meditation.

Sanskrit   The literary language of classic Hindu scriptures.

Sant   A Sikh holy person.

Santeria   A new religious movement with roots in Yoruba religion, which combines orisa with Catholic practices. Developed in Cuba and spread throughout the Caribbean and into the United States.

Saoshyant   Prophet or reformer who pre-Zoroastrian Aryans believed came to restore the purity of religion.

Sarah   Abraham's wife (originally Sarai), who traveled with him to Canaan. Promised many progeny by God, Sarah could not bear children, so she gave her Egyptian maid Hagar to Abraham, who bore him Ishmael. In old age Sarah finally gave birth to Isaac (Gen. 17–23).

Satan   Hebrew for "adversary," borrowed from Persian.

Sati (or Suttee)   In traditional Hinduism, a practice wherein the wife immolates herself on the funeral pyre of her dead husband.

Satori   State of enlightenment that one can achieve in Zen Buddhism.

Sattva   The most refined of gunas, white, light, intelligent, and revealing.

Sawm Required Muslim fasting during the month of Ramadan.

Scholasticism A form of medieval Christian thought that built upon religious dogma a system to keep separate and yet reconcile the spheres of religion and philosophy, faith and reason.

School of National Learning Shinto restoration movement during the Tokugawa period.

Scientology New religious movement founded by L. Ron Hubbard (1911–1986), emphasizing scientific-type techniques to remove mental and physical disorders and bring spiritual transformation.

Scriptures "Writings," especially those writings which are considered authoritative or sacred by a particular religious community.

Second Coming In Christianity, the expected return of Jesus Christ at the end of history to inaugurate the Kingdom of God on earth.

Second Great Awakening A movement in Christianity that occurred during the early nineteenth-century in America; it was characterized by a feeling-centered approach to religion, powerful conversion experiences, an emphasis on individual conscience, religious revival events, and the motivation of individuals to social action on such issues as women's rights and the abolition of slavery.

Second Vatican Council The twenty-first ecumenical council of the Catholic Church, which was convened by Pope John XXIII and, after his death, presided over by Pope Paul VI. The purpose of the council was to renew the Catholic Church for the modern era by implementing significant developments in liturgy (e.g., authorization of conducting the liturgy in the vernacular rather than only in Latin), in theology (e.g., including an openness to religious freedom), in the role of the bishops, and in the relationship of the Catholic Church to the modern world, to other Christian churches, and to non-Christian religions.

Sect A term used by sociologists to denote religious groups related to mainstream religions (e.g. Christianity), but whose adherents believe represent a more intense commitment than the average adherent to the religion to which they are related (e.g., the Amish or the Jehovah's Witnesses in relation to mainstream Christianity).

Sectarian Characterized by sects; may also imply partisanship between sects.

Secular Having to do with this observable reality, as opposed to the spiritual. Secular religions have nonspiritual, this-worldly ultimacies. Nonreligious aspects of society; worldly.

Secularization Denotes a shift from the religious orientation of a society, an institution, a person, a symbol, etc., to a worldly one; also often the shift of social institutions from religious authority to civil authority.

Seder ("Order") The order of a Jewish service, notably the home ritual during Passover, celebrating the spring Passover remembrance of being liberated from Egyptian slavery by God. It includes recitation of prayers, reading of a special text (Haggadah), sharing special symbolic foods and wine in a festive meal, singing Passover songs, and the concluding cry "Next year in Jerusalem."

See An area under the authority of a Christian bishop or archbishop.

Self-Realization Fellowship Modern religious movement founded in America by Yogananda (1893–1952), teaching various Hindu yogic practices.

Semantics The systematic investigation of the development, and changes in the meaning and form, of language.

Semite A Jew, Arab, or other, of eastern Mediterranean origin.

Separation of church and state A central concept in the development of U.S. government, which seeks to maintain a separation of civil and religious authority in society.

Sephardim Jews who fled from Spain and Portugal and took refuge in the Ottoman Empire. The word "Sephardim" derives from the word for "Spain" in Hebrew. All Jews who did not convert to Christianity were expelled from Spain in 1492. Sephardi Jewish practices were influenced by their association with Spain, and their special language, Ladino, is a combination of Hebrew and Spanish.

Seppuku Ritual suicide by disembowelment (the term hara-kiri means "belly slitting"); dictated for certain dishonors and crimes among the samurai.

Septuagint   A Greek version of the Hebrew Scriptures, dating from the third century B.C.E.

Sepulchre   A burial vault, often made of stone.

Seven heavens   During his traditional visionary "Night Journey," Muhammed was escorted by the angel Gabriel through the gates of seven heavens, where he met Allah, who made daily prayers obligatory for Muslims.

Shabd   The Sikh term for a Name of God that is recited or a hymn from the Guru Granth Sahib, considered the Word of God.

Shahadah   The Muslim formula bearing witness to the unity of God. Creedal statement of Islam, "There is no God but God, and Muhammad is the messenger of God."

Shakti   Sanskrit for "power, energy"; in Hinduism, the active energy of a deity, personified as a goddess. Shaktism is the practice of seeking to identify with this active power and draw upon it for material or spiritual pursuits.

Shakyamuni   "Sage of the Shakyas," a title of the Buddha: the wise one of the Shakya clan. One of the titles applied to Gautama Siddhartha as a historical personage.

Shaman   In an indigenous religion, a holy person who through special initiation has powers of spirit-control, divination, healing, and contacting the gods and spirits, usually exercised through elaborate performances and in a trance state.

Shamanism   The experiences and practices of the shaman. It is not an institutionalized religion, but it denotes the use of magic, the entering altered states of consciousness, and the use of techniques to induce lucid dreaming, possession, and out-of-body experiences, all of which may have religious implications.

Shang Ti   Chinese for "Ruler on High"; central deity in ancient Chinese mythology, guarantor of the moral order and of rulers' authority.

Shankara   Great philosopher of Advaita (nondual) Vedanta (788–820 C.E.).

Sharia   The path or way Muslims are to follow; hence, Muslim "law."

Shavuot "Feast of Weeks"; Jewish holiday in remembrance of the giving of the Ten Commandments.

Shaykh A Sufi, or a mystical Islamic, spiritual teacher and guide.

Shekhinah God's presence in the world, in Judaism.

Shema Deuteronomy 6:4, "Hear (shema) O Israel: The Lord our God is one Lord; and you shall love the Lord your God with all your heart, and with all your soul, and with all your might."

Shen Dao Shen Tao, Legalist and Daoist, emphasized natural tendencies and rank, over talent and wisdom: "Let us be like creatures."

Shen In Chinese tradition, heavenly yang spirits; benevolent and honored spirits, including ancestors.

Sheol Hebrew word for the place of the dead.

Shi Power as rank, position, or natural circumstance (as distinguished from law or talent).

Shi Huang Di Qin dynasty, "First Emperor," who unified China under severe totalitarian rule, 221 B.C.E.

Shi Jing Confucian Classic: the Book of Poetry.

Shi`a Islam The "party" of Ali; the minority, some 10 to 15 percent of all Muslims, who traditionally believe that Islam should be headed by a Divinely guided Imam who is a hereditary successor of the Prophet through Ali, Muhammad's cousin. The Shi'ites maintain that Ali, the fourth of the caliphs, was the first Imam, the rightful successor of Muhammad as leader of the Umma or Islamic community. Shi'ites are the dominant Islamic community in Iran.

Shimenawa Straw rope from which tassels and gohei shapes hang, used to make sacred sites and objects.

Shingon Buddhism Esoteric (Tantric) Buddhism in Japan. The form of Buddhism founded by Kobo Daishi (773–835), who was interested in the synthesis of Daoism, Confucianism, and Buddhism. He studied Tantric Buddhism and the Great Sun Sutra in China and then returned to Japan to establish a great monastery on Mount Koya, where esoteric practices were used.

Shingon (Chinese: Zhen-yan) "True word," an esoteric or a mystical sect introduced in Japan by Kukai (Kobo Daishi) in the ninth century.

Shinko shukyo (or Shin-shin-shukyo) Japanese term for the new Japanese religions; literally, "newly arisen religions."

Shinran Founder (1173–1262) Of Jodo Shinshu, True Pure Land Buddhism, in Japan.

Shinto (Shen Tao) Literally, "the way of the gods" (the Japanese language equivalent is Kamino-michi); the native religion of Japan.

Shirk The sin of believing in any divinity except the one God, in Islam.

Shiva One of three major gods of Hinduism (with Brahman and Vishnu); god of energy, violence, and king of the dance, associated with cobras. Husband of Durga, Parvati, and others.

Shivaite (also Shaivite) Devotee of the god Shiva.

Shogatsu Japanese holiday celebrating the New Year.

Shogun In Japan, a hereditary military ruler, ostensibly under the authority of the emperor, but who held nearly complete control over the nation until 1867, when the rule of the Shoguns ended.

Shotoku Prince regent (573–621) who advocated Buddhism as one of the pillars of Japan.

Shrine (jinja) Shinto sacred place focused on the presence of a kami; usually has appropriate buildings where a symbol of the kami is housed and where worshipers can consult priests.

Shruti "That which is heard," the eternal truth, that is, the Vedas.

Shu Jing Confucian Classic: the Book of History.

Shu, mutuality Confucian law of reciprocity. altruism, the art of conducting affairs and managing subordinates.

Shudras Classical servant class in Hindu society, the fourth class.

Siddha   A perfected one, a being who has obtained moksha.

Siddhartha Gautama   The Buddha.

Siddha-sila Jaina   "Home of the perfected ones" under the dome at the apex of the universe.

Sikhism   A religion that originated in the Punjab region of north India in the sixteenth century C.E. as an offshoot of a *bhakti* cult of Hinduism. The word *Sikh* is derived from both Pali and Sanskrit and means "disciple." The Sikhs are the disciples of 10 *gurus* beginning with Nanak (1469–1539) and ending with Gobind Singh (1666–1708). The fifth *guru*, Arfan (1563–1606), consolidated the Sikh community, broke its connections with the Hindus and Muslims, and set it on its own course.

Sikh   Sanskrit for "disciple"; the followers of Guru Nanak.

Sinai   A mountain range in the Negev desert south of Israel.

Singhs   In Sikhism, a corps of warriors.

Sinicize   To make something Chinese.

Sister Emmanuel   A Roman Catholic nun known for teaching poor children in India.

Skandhas   Basic constituents of reality in Buddhist thought; five of them-form, sense, perception, reactions, and consciousness-make up a human being.

Slave morality   Nietzsche's term for moralities that exalt values based on weakness, such as forgiveness and humility. Such moralities, he thought, do not allow for the development of great cultures.

Smriti   "That which is remembered," secondary level of sacred writings that derive from revelation but are composed by human authors.

Social gospel   A movement that strove to correlate religion to new ideas in science and society and to recover the old dream of making America into a new "people of God" through social reform.

Sociological form of religious expression   A religion's forms of group life, leadership, relation to outside society, governance, and interpersonal relations. To find a religion's sociological expression, start by asking yourself, "How do the people involved relate to each other?" and "How are they organized?"

Soka Gakkai   A modernizing lay Buddhist movement in Japan, an outgrowth of the Nichiren sect, politically activist through the Komeito party.

Sola fide/sola scriptura   Luther's view that salvation is based on "faith alone," rather than works, and that authority in the Church is based on "Scripture alone," rather than ecclesiastically controlled "tradition"; the availability of these two sources to individuals led to the Reformation view of the priesthood of all believers.

Soma   "Sacred drink"; sacred plant whose juice was a libation to the gods of India.

Son of Heaven   Title of Chinese emperor.

Song (Sung) Dynasty (1127–1279 B.C.E.)   A period in Chinese history whose society was the first to print books. As a result, there was considerable educational development in this era, and the famous civil service examination system was developed, permitting the rise to status in society of men by merit rather than merely by "connections."

Soto   School of Zen Buddhism that developed in Japan during the Kamakura period (1185–1333), which taught that the way to enlightenment is through lengthy meditation sessions.

Soul   The principle of life and consciousness, commonly believed to have a destiny separate from the physical body.

Spenta Mainyu   Holy Spirit in Zoroastrianism, closely identified with Ahura Mazda, creator of world, opponent of Angra Mainyu.

Spiritual   Referring to a level of existence beyond the ordinary, material, temporal reality of this world. In contrast to "secular" reality.

Spiritualism   A religious movement begun in America in the 1840s, that holds that there is continuity of life and, therefore, there is no death; practices include contact with the spirits of the departed through mediumship. Some groups are organized as Spiritualist Churches.

Srauta sacrifice In Hinduism, great public sacrifice in ancient India.

St. John the Divine Cathedral The Episcopal Cathedral of New York State, in New York City. Gothic architecture, located on Morningside Heights at 110th St, and Cathedral Avenue, between Columbia University and Harlem.

State church The officially recognized church of the governing authority of a nation.

Sthanakvasis Jaina sect that worships without images or temples.

Stigmata Marks of the nails on the hands and feet, of the crown of thorns, and of the stab-wounded side of Christ on the cross, which have been experienced by some ardent Christians.

Stupa Memorial Buddhist shrine or bell-shaped reliquary, usually topped by an umbrella spire; burial mound for a holy person; a sacred site in Buddhism, a focal point for devotion and circumambulation.

Subjectivism In ethics the view that ethical statements are descriptions of the way people feel about certain actions. According to subjectivism, there are no moral standards independent of human feelings.

Sufficient reason The principle that holds that things do not happen without a cause or without some reason sufficient to explain their happening. The principle of sufficient reason cannot be proved but has been suggested as a basic presupposition of all thought.

Sufi Literally, "woolen"; One who follows the mystical path of Islam. A Muslim mystic who teaches that salvation comes through a personal union with Allah and sometimes expresses views differing significantly from mainstream Islamic teachings; devotion often expressed in intense, passionate poetry.

Sukkot Feast of Booths, autumn harvest festival in Judaism.

Summa Theologiae Massive systematic theology by Thomas Aquinas, which became the standard for Catholic theology.

Sun dance Oglala Lakota ritual of rejuvenation.

Sun Zhongshan Founder of the Republic of China (1912); sought a blend of socialist democracy and Confucian morality.

Sun-god Divine being manifested through the sun, important especially in ancient Egypt.

Sunnah "Custom" or "way of acting," primarily of the Prophet Muhammad; the Prophet's sunnah is known through the hadiths.

Sunnis One of the two great sects of Islam, followers of the tradition (*sunna*)—as found in the life and teachings of the Prophet Muhammad—and the *Qur'an* as the authoritative sources. The Sunni represent a moderate, centrist position and is the largest of the sectarian Islamic communities.

Sunyata "Emptiness," the Void, an equivalent to Nirvana, reality stripped of all attributes experienced in samsara.

Superego One of the three functional parts (with the id and ego) of the human personality as understood by Freud; originates in the child's identification with parents and others and serves as an internal censor of behavior. Embraces both the conscious and the unconscious conscience.

Surah One of the divisions (chapters) of the Qur'an.

Susanoo Storm kami in Japanese mythology, unruly brother of Amaterasu.

Susa-no-wo "Valiant Male," brother of Amaterasu, in the Kojiki (assembled by priests of her cult), he appears as a mischief-, pollution-, and storm-causing adversary; his cult was associated with the Izumo shrine.

Sutras Collections of aphorisms, sayings.

suttee In India, the act or custom of burning a live widow on her husband's funeral pyre or burying her alive in his grave. At the insistence of Christians and Hindus, the British government outlawed the practice in 1829.

Svadharma In Hinduism, one's person dharma; one's place in the "great dance" of the social order.

Svetambara Literally, "the white clad"; the more liberal sect of Jainism.

Sweat lodge Special lodge among some Native Americans constructed for purification ceremonies.

Symbol Any object, word, or action which points toward and allows experience of and/or participation in perceived ultimacy, evoke deep meanings by connecting with sacred reality.

Sympathetic or imitative magic Magic that seeks to operate on the basic notion that look-alikes act alike. The voodoo doll and the various rain dances that incorporate the sprinkling of water or the imitation of thunder are examples.

Synagogue "Gathering of people" Jewish local center of prayer, reading Scripture, and hearing teachings led by a rabbi. The synagogue gained importance in the diaspora, after the destruction of Jerusalem's temple in 70 C.E.

Syncretism In religion, the effort to bring together into a synthesis or harmony different beliefs or practices from several religious traditions to create a new union.

Synod In Christianity, a council of church officials called to reach agreement on doctrines and administration.

Synoptic Gospels The first three Gospels of the New Testament. Believed by most scholars to have been written between 65 and 85 C.E. They are called "synoptic" (derived from synopsis, which in Greek means "view together") because they are thought to be related to each other in terms of sources and meaning in ways that the Gospel of John, the fourth Gospel, is not.

Synthetic Refers to those kinds of statements in which the predicate adds something not already contained in the subject. The truth or falsity of synthetic statements is determined by observation and sense experience.

Systematics The techniques of using exegesis, history, and other tools to set out a comprehensive account of the beliefs of a particular community.

Ta'ziya "Lamentation," a Shi'ite passion play reenacting events centered upon the martyrdom of al-Hoseyn (Arabic: al-Husayn) at Karbala.

Tabernacle A moveable shrine in which Yahweh was worshipped by the Hebrews until Solomon built a great temple; it contained the written Torah. Its design and method of construction were given by God to Moses at Mount Sinai.

Taboo English form of the Polynesian word meaning "marked off" or "prohibited"; associated with a sacred— that is, dangerous—object or person who is not to be touched or approached for fear of supernatural contagion.

Tai Ji The Great Ultimate, the supreme regulative principle of the cosmos; li acting through qi.

Tai Wu Di Fifth-century Northern Wei emperor, made Daoism the official religion of his realm.

T'ai-chi chu'an An ancient Chinese system of physical exercises, which uses slow movements to help one become part of the universal flow of energy.

Taiping Rebellion Abortive popular movement in the mid-nineteenth century in China, based on religious ideas, attempting to change the hierarchical structure of society.

Taj Mahal Muslim mausoleum in Agra India (1630–52 C.E.), built by Shah Jahan for his deceased wife Mumtaz Mahal.

Talisman A magical object that is believed to guarantee good fortune, health, and other benefits. A talisman is often worn concealed on the person or in a dwelling. They are the counterpart of amulets that are used to protect against disease or evil.

Talit A shawl traditionally worn by Jewish men during prayers.

Talmud From Hebrew, meaning "learning" or "teaching"; an encyclopedic collection of the Jewish oral law consisting of the Mishnah and Gemara. Compiled between the first century and the end of the fifth century C.E., it is the highest legal authority in Judaism after the five books of the written Torah.

Tamas The dark guna, inert, dull, and heavy.

Tammuz (Adonis) A Mesopotamian god of vegetation and fertility; cultic veneration of him by Hebrew women is mentioned in the Book of Ezekiel.

Tanak An acronym from the Hebrew names for the three sections of the Hebrew Bible-Torah, Prophets, Writings; used as a designation for the Hebrew Bible.

Tang Dynasty A period (618–907 C.E.) in Chinese history of great learning and cultural sophistication admired by many foreigners; the arts flourished and China had considerable military power.

Tanha Desire, thirst, or craving; a concept identified by Buddha as that which causes karma.

Tantra Sanskrit for "that which extends, spreads." In a broad sense, tantrism is a religious practice outside the Vedic tradition, including rituals open to persons not of the Brahmin class. Practiced in Hinduism, Tibetan Buddhism, and Jainism, tantrism attempts to harness corporeal energy, ultimately for the highest spiritual purposes.

Tantras Manuals that teach magical words and spells, primarily found in Tibetan Buddhism but also present in other Buddhist sects and in Hinduism, where tantric religion takes on the element of enlightenment by carrying passion to extremes.

Tao Also Dao the "way" or "power" of harmony and balance among all things. The term is also used as a name for the Nameless.

Tao Tê Ching Literally, "The Classic of the Way and its Power or Virtue"; the book that became the basis for the philosophy of Taoism.

Taoism (or "Daoism") The major Chinese religion/philosophy that complements Confucianism. Traditionally founded by Lao-Tzu and the *Tao te Ching* text, Taoism stresses inward awareness, not just behavior. The Tao is the inexpressible unproduced producer of existence, the primordial source of order, yet concealed and full of paradox. Influenced Buddhism, especially Zen.

Tapas Austerity-generated "heat"; subjectively, each impulse mastered stokes the inner fire of psychic power; universally, containment generates warmth incubating the cosmic germ/egg.

Tariqa   In Islam, an esoteric Sufi order.

Tatarstan   Muslim region in southern Russia between Chechnya, Kyrgyzstan, and Moscow.

Tathagata   "One who has gone thus" or "come thus"-a title of the Buddha emphasizing his passing from worldly existence into Nirvana.

Tautology   A statement that is logically or trivially true by virtue of its meaning.

Tawaf   The ritualistic circling of the Ka'bah cube seven times at the center of the Great Mosque in Mecca.

Tawhid   Muslim term for maintaining the unity of God.

Teleological   From the Greek word for end or purpose; refers to that which is purposive. Teleological arguments for God's existence are based on the claim that the world exhibits order and purpose, which can best be explained with reference to God.

Teleological suffering   Suffering that accomplishes some purpose, as opposed to dysteleological suffering, which is suffering with no apparent purpose.

Temple of 1,000 Pillars   One among many beautiful richly-carved temples in India, the Chandranath temple in Mudbidri, Karnataka, near Bangalore on the south-west coast, has 1,000 pillars.

Ten Commandments   The first of the 613 laws of the Jewish Torah, in Exodus 20. Some are theological ("You shall have no other gods before me"), and some ethical ("You shall not kill").

Ten Plagues   When Moses returned from Midian to Egypt and urged Pharaoh to free his Hebrew slaves, Pharaoh repeatedly refused. So by tradition told in Exodus 7–12, God sent ten plagues to punish Egypt until Pharaoh released the Hebrews. Nile and well water turned to blood, fish died, and water turned foul. "But the magicians of Egypt did the same by their secret arts" says Exodus 7:22, so Pharaoh was not convinced. Then frogs hopped into houses, gnats and flies swarmed, cattle died, boils covered Egyptians, thunder and hail harmed crops, locusts devoured crops, darkness fell for three days, and the first born children of the Egyptians died, while the Hebrews escaped.

Tendai Buddhism   The form of Buddhism founded by Dengyo Daishi (762–822), who held that the Lotus Sutra is the final and culminating expression of the Buddha's teaching. Dengyo Daishi studied Tiantai Buddhism in China and then returned to Japan to establish a great monastery on Mount Hiei, which became a most significant influence on the spiritual history of Japan.

Tenrikyo ("Religion of Heavenly Wisdom")   The oldest of the modern New Religions of Japan, founded in 1838; a charismatic revelation in 1838 turned Nakayama Miki into a "living kami" who spread the healing power of the Heavenly Parent, Tenri O no Mikoto.

T'fillin   A small leather box with verses about God's covenant with the Jewish people, bound to the forehead and arm.

Theocratic   Of or under a theocracy—the rule of a state or a society by God or by priests or God's representatives who claim to rule by divine authority.

Theodicy   From the Greek *theos* ("god") and *dike* ("justice"); introduced by the philosopher Leibniz to designate the problem of justifying the goodness and power of God in view of the evil in the world. Used more broadly by social scientists to describe any legitimation of an ideology or world view in the face of the threat of chaos and meaninglessness.

Theology   Believing reflection on the faith of a particular community, with the goal of clarification of the logic and grounds of a notion of the sacred.

Theophany   A manifestation or appearance of the divine at a definite time and a definite place. Moses' experience of the burning bush was an example of a theophany.

Theoretical form of religious expression   A religion's stories, concepts, ideas, doctrines. To find a religion's theoretical expression, start by asking yourself, "What do they say?"

Theragatha   Psalms of the male elders.

Theravada   An early Hinayana sect that survives today; term generally used for the type of Buddhist tradition and practice followed in South and Southeast Asia

Therigatha Translates as "Psalms of the Sisters." This is a collection of beautiful accounts of the enlightenment of over 70 women who are believed to have been among the first nuns of Buddhism.

Thich Nhat Hanh A 20th-21st century Zen Buddhist monk from Vietnam, living in Plum Village France, who has written numerous influential books, such as *No Death, No Fear*.

Third Adam According to the teaching of the Unification Church, a messiah who will appear to pay the full price for the sin of humanity and establish the Kingdom of God on earth; Jesus was the second Adam.

Three Ages of the Dharma Buddhist teaching of increasing decline and degeneracy in humans' ability to follow the Buddhist path: the Age of the Perfect Dharma, the Age of the Counterfeit Dharma, and the Age of the End of the Dharma.

Three Body Teaching Mahayana teaching of three dimensions of the Buddha: the Dharma Body, the Bliss Body, and the Transformation Body.

Three Pure Ones Designation for highest gods summoned by Daoist priests.

Three Refuges or Three Jewels The Buddha as the ideal teacher; the Dharma as his teaching or "gospel," and the Samgha, or order of monks, as the ideal community-three ideals that a person affirms on formally becoming a Buddhist or a Buddhist monk or nun.

Tian Chinese word usually translated as "heaven," but means also the supreme ruler or moderator of the universe who gives rain, victory, fortune or misfortune, and who regulates the moral order.

Tiantai (or T'ien T'ai) A school of Mahayana Buddhism in China, based on the Lotus Sutra.

Tibetan Book of the Dead The book that is Tibet's most famous contribution to the world's religious thought. It sets out an account of the experiences of a deceased person after death. Also known as the Bardo Thodol.

Tirthankara "Ford builder," Jain idea of one who has reached total liberation and shows the way across the ocean of suffering.

Tirthankaras Literally, "ford-finders," the twenty-four Jaina hero Siddhas who showed the way to moksha.

Tonsure The rite of clipping the hair or shaving the head to denote admission of a candidate to a religious order, often to a life of a monk.

Torah Hebrew for "instruction, law"; God's revelation of instructions to the Jewish people. First five books in the Hebrew scriptures; also the whole of scripture; also the whole corpus of revelation, including oral Torah.

Torii The gently curved archway that leads into the precincts of a Shinto shrine.

Totemism Adopted from the Ojibwa Indian language for the widespread practice of associating human tribes or classes with animals or plants, from which the group is descended or has some close relationship. Some writers claim that the group worships the totem animal and that totemism is the earliest form of religion. These theories are now widely disputed.

Tradition "Passing on" of the sacred story and basic ideas of a religion.

Transcendent Literally means "that which goes beyond"; in religion the transcendent refers to that which lies beyond the physical or natural order. The traditional Jewish, Christian, and Islamic view is that God is a transcendent being.

Transcendental Meditation Hindu meditation movement founded in America by Maharishi Mahesh Yogi (b. 1917), emphasizing simple meditation techniques for practical benefits.

Transfiguration The story in the Gospels (Mark 9:2, etc.) of Jesus at a mountaintop with disciples, taking on a glorious light-filled appearance, alongside Moses and Elijah.

Transformation Reaching the ideal state of wholeness, perfection, or salvation.

Transmigration The movement of a soul or spirit from one existence to another.

Transpersonal Referring to an eternal, infinite reality, in contrast to the finite material world.

Transubstantiation In many branches of Christianity, the belief that through the proper consecration during the sacrament of Holy Communion the elements of bread and wine become the substance of the body and blood of Christ.Eastern Orthodox and Protestant churches (not committed to a substance philosophy) use more mystical and metaphoric language to describe the real presence of Christ in the Eucharist.

Trikaya The three "bodies" or forms of expression of the Buddha-nature.

Trinity The doctrine that there are three "persons," the Father, the Son (Christ), and the Holy Spirit, in the one God.

Tripitaka The oldest Buddhist scriptures. The scriptures of the Pali Canon of Buddhism, meaning "Three Baskets"; they include the Vinaya Pitaka, the Sutra Pitaka, and the Abhidharma Pitaka. They are the only ones considered authoritative by Theravada Buddhism.

True Name The Sikh name for the one God.

Tsumi Impurity or misfortune, a quality that Shinto purification practices are designed to remove.

Tudigong (T'u Ti Kung) Local earth god in Chinese religion.

Tunkashila Oglala Lakota word for "grandfather." In prayers, Wakan Tanka is often addressed as Tunkashila.

Tushita heaven A celestial dwelling place of "satisfied ones" (bodhisattvas) during their next-to-last existence-a part of this world as distinguished from remote, timeless, Buddha fields.

Twelvers (Ashariyah) The majority of Shi'ites, who accept the first twelve of the Imams in the line of Ali, believing that the Twelfth has gone into hiding to return as the Mahdi, or messianic savior, who will establish a paradisal reign on earth just before the end of the world and the judgment.

Typology The study of types—for example, of religious phenomena such as forms of sacrifice and types of deity.

Tzaddik An enlightened Jewish mystic.

Udasi   An ascetic Sikh order.

Udasis   Order of holy men in Sikhism.

Ulama   Collective term for Muslim religious scholars and teachers who, by consensus, establish correct teaching, scholars responsible for interpreting Sharia.

Ullambana ("The Festival of Souls")   A Buddhist festival celebrated in China and Japan; worshiping the souls of ancestors and providing for souls temporarily released from purgatory;. Families leave gifts of food for the souls of their departed ancestors thought to be wandering the earth. Called Obon in Japan.

'Umar   The second caliph in Islamic history (d. 644).

Umayyad   Dynasty ruling Islam from Damascus from 661 to 750 C.E.

Umma   Arabic for "community"; often used for the entire community of Muslims throughout the world.

Unconditioned reality   The opposite of conditioned reality; reality in its absolute nature equally present in all times and places and not limited in any way.

Unification Church   A group founded by the Rev. Sun Myung Moon, which combines Christian, shamanistic, and messianic features. Its adherents are often referred to pejoratively as "Moonies."

Univocal   The use of language in which a term has one and only one meaning, or at least one central meaning in terms of which its various usages can be understood.

Untouchables   The Hindu social category of people outside the caste system, forbidden to marry, eat, or work with higher caste members. Education and reading sacred texts is forbidden. They must live outside villages, work at impure occupations, such as scavenging or funerals. Also known as the "scheduled castes." Mahatma Gandhi called the untouchables harijan, children of God. Increasingly, they are known as dalits, oppressed ones.Officially abolished by India's modern constitution, but informally still practiced.

Upanishads   The last and most philosophical of the Vedas, centering around the message that Atman is Brahman; one's true self is the universal Divine Reality.

Upaya "Skill-in-means," compassion in action, the complement of prajna; in Tantric Buddhism, the male consort in symbolic coupling.

Uposatha Fortnightly Buddhist holy day when temple meetings for teaching, ritual, and meditation are held.

Ushas White-robed goddess of the dawn; eternally young, she rides a chariot driven by her male attendants, the twin Asvins.

Usury The exacting of interest on a loan or debt. Before the rise of modern capitalism, Judaism, Christianity, and Islam forbade the practice of usury (see Exodus 22:25; Deuteronomy 23:19f) from biblical times through the Middle Ages and even beyond.

'Uthman The third caliph in Islamic history (d. 656).

Utilitarian A philosophical and ethical position that identifies right ethical actions with the effort to maintain the greatest good and happiness for the greatest number of people. It arose in the late eighteenth century and in the early and mid-nineteenth century; it was very influential and associated with the English philosophers Jeremy Bentham and John Stuart Mill.

Utopian A view that envisions an ideal or near-perfect world or social order. The word was first used by Sir Thomas More in his book *Utopia* (1516) and derived from the Greek meaning "no place." It was, however, used to suggest a good or ideal place. In religion, utopian prophecies are often associated with messianic-millenarian groups who look to the overthrow of the evil powers and the coming of a new and ideal social order here on earth.

Vairocana "Shining out," celestial Dhyani Buddha of Effulgent Light (the sun), the center in the Tantric set of five; as Dainichi "Great Sun" in Japan, his body, speech, and mind pervade the universe.

Vaisheshika Hindu philosophical system that teaches that the universe is made up of nine distinct and uncreated elements.

Vaishnavite (or Vaishnava) A Hindu devotee of Vishnu, particularly in his incarnation as Krishna.

Vaishyas The classical producer-merchant caste in Hindu society

Vajrayana Diamond Vehicle, the Tantric tradition of Buddhism, represented especially in Tibet and Japan.

Varnas Major groupings of castes in Hinduism; literally, "colors." The four main varnas are (1) brahmins or priests; (2) kshatriyas or rulers and warriors; (3) vaishyas or craftsmen and merchants; and (4) shudras or farmers and peasants. Harijans or untouchables are not one of the varnas, as they are outcasts.

Varuna Vedic god of the heavens.

Vatican II Council called by the Roman Catholic Church in 1962; it took broad steps to modernize the Church and mend relationships with Jews, members of the Eastern Orthodox Church, and Protestants.

Vedanta Literally, "the end of the Vedas"; this Hindu philosophical system takes its major materials from the Upanishads and assumes that there is only one true reality in the world Brahman.

Vedanta Societies Hindu groups in America and Europe following the teaching of Swami Vivekananda (1863–1902) and Sri Ramakrishna (1836–1886).

Vedas Sanskrit for "knowledge"; the sacred writings of the Aryans, deemed canonical by later Hinduism. Basic collections include hymns to the gods (Rig-Veda), ritual materials and directions for the sacrifices and invocations for the gods (Yajur-Veda), verses from the Rig-Veda arranged musically (Sama-Veda), and hymns together with spells and incantations (Atharva-Veda).

Verification principle A principle suggested by A. J. Ayer by means of which to distinguish meaningful statements from nonsense. According to the verification principle, a statement is meaningful if, and only if, it is analytic or can in principle be verified empirically.

Via negativa "The way of the negative"; especially a use of language wherein one makes only negative statements, not positive ones, in order to avoid possible equivocation in language usage. Examples would be to say that God is not finite, or God is not evil.

Vinaya Texts containing rules for Buddhist monastic life and discipline.

Vipassana Theravada method of meditation that aims at analyzing one's experience until one realizes that conditioned reality is impermanent, unsatisfactory, and has no "self."

Vishnu One of the major devotional gods of bhakti. Vishnu is God as the force on behalf of order and righteousness. He descends from the highest heaven in incarnate form whenever righteousness declines, working to restore good in the world. Krishna is a descent of Vishnu.

Vision quest Native American tradition involving individual purification and several days of fasting and praying in a remote sacred place to attain spiritual powers and direction for life.

Vohu Manah The mode of Good Thought or Sense; appeared to Zoroaster as an archangel and led him to the presence of Ahura Mazda.

Voodoo Latin American and Caribbean ways of working with the spirit world, a blend of West African and Catholic Christian teachings.

Vulgate Latin translation of the Bible by Jerome.

Wahhabi Ultraconservative Muslim movement founded in the eighteenth century and opposed to all forms of change within religion and culture.

Wahhabism The teachings of the Arab Theologian Muhammad ibn 'Abd al-Wahhab, which insisted on a purification of and renewal of Islam by strict adherence to the authentic Islam of the founding prophet Muhammad. It has profoundly influenced contemporary Sunni Islamic traditionalists and Fundamentalists.

Wakan Oglala Lakota for "holy" or "sacred." Wakana is "holiness." A wicasa wakan is a holy man; a winyan wakan is a holy woman (shaman). Wakan Tanka is the Great Mystery.

Wang Chong First-century C.E. rationalist, opposed supernaturalism and excessive reverence for Confucius the man.

Wang Yangming A leading Neo-Confucianist (1472–1529) who taught that the principle of the myriad separate things is actually within the mind itself, and therefore the supreme requisite is sincerity of mind. Also known as Wang Shouren.

Wat Complex of buildings used in Theravada Buddhism for worship and teaching.

Way of art In Japan, practice of an art (such as poetry, Noh drama, or the tea ceremony) as a way of self-cultivation.

Weltanschauung The German term for worldview.

Whirling Dervish A type of Muslim Sufi, the Mevlevi Order of mystics who dance in a circular whirl to achieve an ecstatic trance and experience Allah.

White Buffalo Calf Woman Oglala Lakota mythic figure who brought the sacred pipe to the people and instructed them in how to live harmoniously.

Wicca Old English for "wise." A New Age feminist movement that has adapter pre-Christian religious witchcraft practices into a benevolent religion oriented toward the harnessing of the feminine principle and energy present in nature for healing and social betterment.

Word, or Word of God (1) Jesus Christ as manifestation of God; (2) the Scripture understood as directly revealed by God. (An emphasis on the "Word" aspect of Christianity usually entails an emphasis on Scripture, preaching, and a relation of inward faith to Jesus Christ.). (3) Word of God in Sikh thought, God's presence that reverberates throughout creation, channeled especially through the gurus.

Worship Respectful ritual activity in special times, directed toward sacred beings or realities of ultimate value.

Wu Di Second-century B.C.E. Han emperor, patron of Confucianism as well as of Daoist alchemy and geomancy.

Wu-wei In Daoism, nonbeing or not doing; not a "thing" or a "cause," but just the spontaneous flow in an endless stream of flux and change. The Dao is of this nature; person who lives this way is in synchronism with the Dao.

Xian   Daoist sage immortals.

Xiao   Filial piety, in later Confucianism, "the source of all virtues."

Xin   Good faith; one of the Five Virtues.

Xunzi (Hsün Tzu)   Important Confucian thinker (ca. 300–238 B.C.E.) who advocated a realistic understanding of the human inclination toward evil. Claimed that man is basically evil in the sense of being self-centered and, therefore, needs education and social control to become good.

Yahweh Special covenant name of Israel's God as it was probably pronounced; written YHWH in the Hebrew scriptures; at a certain point Jews stopped pronouncing this sacred name and substituted the name Adonai.

Yantra In Tantric Hinduism and Buddhism, a linear cosmic symbol used as an aid to spiritual concentration. Used in meditation.

Yarmulke Skull cap worn by Jewish males at worship.

Yasht Song of praise, a portion of the Avesta.

Yasna Liturgical scripture, written in Gathic (Old Persian); includes the Gathas.

Yazata Worshipful ones, Indo-Iranian gods who continued to be objects of worship in Zoroastrianism, sometimes called angels.

Yi Righteous conduct (as opposed to conduct motivated by desire for personal profit), a Confucian virtue stressed by Mencius.

Yiddish The language of Ashkenazi Jews. Essentially, it is Middle High German written in the Hebrew alphabet, spoken in Jewish communities of Eastern Europe (the Ashkenazim).

Yijing The Classic of Changes, an ancient Chinese divination manual based on sixty-four hexagrams (each of six unbroken and broken lines).

Yin-Yang The two complementary, opposite forces present in all reality, according to the traditional thought that interact and give birth to the universe. They are not separate, but flow into each other. Yin is traditionally the feminine, yielding, receptivity, moon, and water. Yang is seen in the masculine, hard, active, red, sun, and upward-thrusting. Traditional Chinese art always includes both in harmony, as in a picture of a mountain with a lake at its base.

Yogacara The "mind only" or "consciousness only" school in Mahayana Buddhism; also called the Vijnanavada; taught by the brothers Asanga and Vasubandhu.

Yoga Sanskrit for "to yoke or join"; refers to a variety of methods that seek to join the individual soul (atman) to the Ultimate, and thus achieve liberation from rebirth.

Yogi One who practices Yoga (Sanskrit: "yoking" or "joining" to the divine) and purifying the self. Various methods include *Hatha Yoga* (bodily postures), *Karma Yoga* (work without attachment to results), *Bhakti Yoga* (devotion to a deity in worship), *Jnana Yoga* (knowledge through study) and *Raja Yoga* (meditation). Some yogis undertake ascetic practices.

Yom Kippur In Judaism, the Day of Atonement, which follows ten days after Rosh Hashana, and which is commemorated by fasting and prayer.

Yoni In Hinduism, a circular sacred image representative of the female reproductive organ, often associated with the lingam.

Yoruba A tribal people living in Nigeria.

Zakat   The alms-tax charitable obligation, third of the "Five Pillars" of Islamic duty—in general terms, one-fortieth of accumulated wealth, though rules are often complex.

Zao Jun (Tsao Chun)   God of the Cooking Stove in Chinese religion.

Zarathustra   The founder of Zoroastrianism, who lived perhaps around 1000 B.C.E., reformed the Indo-Aryan religion, and composed the Gathas.

Zazen   Zen Buddhist sitting meditation.

Zealots   An ultranationalistic Jewish sect in Palestine who led the first war against Rome in 67–68 C.E.; disappeared after the fall of Jerusalem (70 C.E.). Also called sicarii ("dagger men") or lestai ("brigands") by their critics.

Zen Rock Garden   A gravel and rock rectangular field at a Zen temple or monastery, notably at the Ryonji temple in Kyoto, Japan, where the gravel is raked smooth and fifteen larger rocks are placed in groups of seven, five, and three, so that from any one view, one rock is hidden.

Zen (Chinese: Ch'an)   A Chinese and Japanese Buddhist school emphasizing that all things have Buddha-nature, which can only be grasped when one escapes from the intellectual mind.

Zend Avesta   The scriptures of Zoroastrianism. Although it contains the Gathas (hymns ascribed to Zoroaster himself), there is much material of a later and more priestly character.

Zendo   A Zen meditation hall.

Zeus   Sovereign over the Olympian gods in ancient Greece.

Zhen Zong   Song emperor; his fabricated "messages from Heaven" equated the Jade Emperor with Shang Di.

Zheng-ming   Rectification of names, making actuality conform to defined ideals.

Zhi   Wisdom; one of the Five Virtues.

Zhong Yong   The Doctrine of the Mean, essay on Confucian ideas of humanity and ethics, a chapter in the Li Ji.

Zhou Dynasty Long dynasty (ca. 1123–221 B.C.E.) during which the classics were compiled and the Confucianist and Daoist traditions developed.

Zhu xi A Neo-Confucianist leader (1130–1200) who taught that the one great ultimate is manifested in the principles of the myriad separate things. Also, known as Chu Hsi.

Zhuangzi The first great Daoist writer (died c. 3000 B.C.E.) to make the potential of Laozi's vision more explicit. In fact, some scholars hold that it is really Zhuangzi who wrote the Dao de jing and who also invented Laozi as a fictional, but representative figure. Also known as Chuang-tzu.

Ziggurat A type of pyramidal structure erected by ancient Mesopotamians, a human-made mountain with stepped-back terracing encased in brick and topped by a shrine.

Zionism Political movement founded in the late nineteenth century by Theodore Herzl; Zionism sought to find a national home for the Jews scattered throughout the world, where all Jews of the world may come and live without fear of persecution.

Zionist Churches Independent Christian groups in Africa that have attempted to combine African traditions with Christianity.

Zoe Greek word meaning "life" that is used by John Hick to refer to spiritual existence. He argues that "soul making" is the transition from bios to zoe.

Zoroaster Greek form of the name Zarathustra.

Zoroastrianism Religious tradition originating in the seventh century B.C.E. in Persia.

Zurvan Boundless Time, or Space-Time, a unitary world principle; a cult of Zurvanism (condemned by the Magi) conceived of him as the "father" of both Ohrmazd and Ahriman.